AT FIRST GLANCE -
What Faces Reveal

(What does your face tell about you?)

Annemarie
Eveland

Library of Congress
Cataloging-in-Publication Data.
Eveland, A. 2011.
(Self-Help and Psychology)
ISBN# 978-1515164142

AT FIRST GLANCE - What Faces Reveal!
(What does your face tell about you?)

Book Cover Design - Artwork
by A. Debra Schwalm

Hurrah For Humans, LLC.
P.O. Box 493
Pine, AZ 85544-0493
USA

Website: http://annemarieeveland.com
Blog: https://annemarieeveland.wordpress.com
Email: Annemarie@HurrahForHumans.com

Dedication

This book is dedicated to all human beings who have struggled to understand, accept and improve themselves. To those special human beings who accept other people without trying to change them, but inspire them to be their best selves, to build bridges between their differences and to celebrate their human spirit.

In a world where our common language separates us, where our feelings and our emotions many times alienate us and beliefs born innocent in childhood oppose whole nations, it is a miracle, indeed, that we find a way to unite, understand, appreciate and love each other.

Such devotion deserves our highest praise and greatest salute to the human spirit. No matter what our physical family genetics, culture, socio-economic and religious background, we are all one spirit expressing differently through our own unique forms. This book shows how we are all differently predisposed, yet inside each of us is that same essence of spirit.

I give my admiration, thanks and support to those who reach out, risk touching, knowing and loving one another.

I dedicate this book to those wonderful people who keep their hearts open when challenged to close down, who believe the best about us when we don't see it, who remember we all have the same heartfelt spirit with our own individual personal exterior packaging.

As you journey through this book, may this information help you to appreciate your beautiful self and know you "can take people at *face* value" when you know how to read their faces, even before they speak.

Acknowledgments

I am appreciative of the help that I received from Deb Schwalm for this book's layout design and completion for publishing.

I am grateful for the background training I have received over the years from my mentor Robert Whiteside for his empirical research to further this science and to the Personology Institute for continuing the teaching of this valuable information.

I also am grateful to friends and family who encouraged me to finish this book; and I thank several writer friends who were willing to give me feedback by reading for me.

I thank my parents, who raised me as one of eleven children in modest surroundings. However, we were richly blessed with values of honesty, caring, respectfulness, kindness and spirituality. They instilled in us honorable values to care for people above things, faith above fashion and family and friends above fame.

In addition, I salute you, the reader of this book, who has taken an interest in learning more about yourself, about other people...before they speak.

Contents

AT FIRST GLANCE — What Faces Reveal 1

Copyright 2

Dedication 3-4

Acknowledgments 5

Contents 6-8

Foreword 9-18

PART ONE
Facial Traits... 19

INTRODUCTION of Facial Traits 20-23

How to Use This Book 24-26

1. Trait of Discriminative 27-33
2. Trait of Analytical 34-43
3. Trait of Emotional Expressiveness44-51
4. Trait of Tolerance.................... 52-55
5. Trait of Self Confidence 56-64
6. Trait of Self Reliance 65-71
7. Trait of Verbal Style 72-81
8. Trait of Physical Insulation 82-91
9. Trait of Administrative 92-100
10. Trait of Thinking Style 101-109
11. Trait of Credulity 110-117

SUMMARY of Facial Traits 118-124

PART TWO
"Trait Talk Stories" 125

INTRODUCTION to "Trait Talk Stories" 126-129

1. Trait of Discriminative 130-134
2. Trait of Analytical 135-141
3. Trait of Emotional Expressiveness 142-145
4. Trait of Tolerance 146-153
5. Trait of Self Confidence 154-158
6. Trait of Self Reliance 159-164
7. Trait of Verbal Style 165-169
8. Trait of Physical Insulation 170-175
9. Trait of Administrative 176-184
10. Trait of Thinking Style 185-190
11. Trait of Credulity 191-197

SUMMARY of "Trait Talk Stories" 198

PART THREE
At-a-Glance Traits 199

INTRODUCTION to At-a-Glance 200-201

1. Trait of Discriminative 202-203
2. Trait of Analytical 204-205

3.   Trait of Emotional Expressiveness 206-207

4.   Trait of Tolerance 208-209

5.   Trait of Self Confidence 210-211

6.   Trait of Self Reliance 212-213

7.   Trait of Verbal Style 214-215

8.   Trait of Physical Insulation 216-217

9.   Trait of Administrative 218-219

10. Trait of Thinking Style 220-221

11. Trait of Credulity 222-223

SUMMARY of At-a-Glance 224-225

Glossary of Traits 226-228

About Author Annemarie 229-231

Contact Annemarie 232

Personal Note Pages

Foreword

Every day we try and read other people. We try to figure out what the other person means by interpreting their words or actions. In every communication, negotiation and relationship there is the spoken and unspoken language. Trying to understand the other person and effectively communicate our meaning to them can be challenging even when we are speaking the same language. Our ability to have shared meaning and successful outcomes is severely limited if we do not know ourselves and cannot read the other person.

What can you tell about a person when you meet for the first time? How well can you read the person *before* they begin to speak? Will they automatically doubt you or accept what you say at face value? Are they interested in money or in human values? Do they need you to quickly get to the bottom line or will they give you time to explain your thoughts more fully? Do they make their decisions from a logical or emotional motivation? Are they very sensitive to their environment or more rugged in their approach to life? Will they require time and space to get to know you or will they become your friend in the first few minutes of meeting you?

These are just a few questions you could quickly answer as the person is walking towards you, simply by glancing at their face! Our physical features speak louder than our words. You can gather immense information about a person simply by looking at their face. It tells you how to communicate with them, treat them so they feel you really understand them, appreciate them and establish instant rapport with them. In that first glance, all this information is known *before* they speak or gesture.

Empirical research has shown a direct correlation between our physical structure and our individual behavior. Our genetic makeup is the basis for predicting our patterns of behavior. People have their own unique genetic blueprint and by observing their structure, you will know a lot about their personality. Although some genetic subgroups have slightly different baselines, within each culture the same degrees of differences are found. Whatever our profession or our personal involvement with another, we are faced with trying establish rapport, communicate more effectively and deepen our relationships every day.

Throughout history, man has observed that in the animal kingdom the animals that were broad-faced, such as the lion and the cobra acted boldly, were not easily intimidated; while the long narrow faced animals such as the deer and the garter snake were easily intimidated, tentative and would retreat quickly. Man recognized a relationship between how the animal was built and how they automatically functioned.

In the human world also, our structure inclines how we will function. Perhaps this method of personality assessment is most effective because its validity is based upon the individual uniqueness of a person's physical structure. It is specific, exact and reveals how each individual thinks feels and will be predisposed to act on automatic. All this can be known about a person – at first glance.

We can easily notice how structure predisposes function by looking at the animal kingdom; for example, the Clydesdale horses that pull the weighty wagonload of beer. These sturdy Clydesdale horses are structured to pull heavy loads, not to run sleek and fast. We would not enter them in the Kentucky Derby nor would we expect the quarter race horse to be successfully pulling the wagonload of beer. Similarly, we do not expect the elephant to run lightly and swiftly like the cheetah, nor think the cheetah would carry the loads assigned to the elephant. How they function follows a natural order of their structure - how they are built to function.

The same is true in our human world. Many of our successful sports athletes are chosen for their fields because their structure is best suited for the activity. The key to understanding ourselves is to understand how we are built to automatically function as our individual self. As human beings, however, we are endowed with "conscious choice" which supersedes our structure. This means that when we are aware of our automatic tendencies and wish to change them, we can. And as we continue to make changes in our behaviors, our physical features also change.

Understanding our own personality through our structure will enable us to choose wisely how to direct those traits which are operating to our detriment. Not knowing our automatic traits may be a hindrance for us, create serious situations and unintended conflicts in our relationships.

Often times our outward expression is misinterpreted. Our personality traits may be naturally opposite from another person, which causes differences in the way we perceive, operate and reflect on life. When we learn to understand the opposites of our *own* personality traits, we are able to gain dominion over them. We can then learn to relate to other people by honoring their traits; by thinking of their interests and from their points of view and speaking in terms that complement their natural communication style.

Choice and dominion are part of the tools we can use to understand ourselves and communicate effectively with others. As we appreciate our individual packaging, we will discover how we have many choices over our automatic actions and thoughts. We are not limited by our structure.

As we come to know our automatic tendencies and make choices of how to direct them, we improve our relationships with all other people in our lives.

This book shows how each of us is uniquely individual as a human being. Regardless of our race, we all have the same traits. The intensity of each trait is different, both in the individuals themselves and between individuals.

Our language often reflects what we instinctively sense about how the other person automatically behaves. We already use terms that show how our physical attributes (our traits) are read by others. Here are some examples. (Since traits are not sex linked, we use pronouns interchangeably.)

When we hear she is "thin-skinned," we know she is more sensitive to her surroundings, physically and emotionally. Everything seems to affect her. He may be "thick skinned" and it will take a lot of all the sensory elements before anything bothers him, appears dense or insensitive.

"He's got a nose for news." There's a person who has that uncanny ability to collect information. He has insatiable curiosity. Some call him nosey.

"She's a high brow." We sense that she is very discriminating, does not appear very friendly or easy to get to know, is selective, and tends to have a reserved attitude; maybe she appears "cold, aloof and unapproachable."

"He's a low brow." Here's a casual man, easily makes friends, not very concerned about appearances, will bring anyone home; makes few distinctions.

"He's thick-headed." He seems a bit dense. It's hard to get through to him.

"She's very tight lipped." She doesn't mince words and speaks very little.

"She's very wishy-washy. Usually these people are not firm with their convictions, are soft in body tone and not very decisive.

Our language itself reflects our knowledge of how people tend to act, think and speak. Each of these terms does relate to a specific physical feature on our faces. These physical features are located in the places we would naturally look for them. For example, our verbal expression features are located around our mouth, our emotional expression traits around our eyes; our thinking traits are located on the upper part of our head, etc. It follows a very natural order.

Do we then become type cast from our traits? No, we are not isolated single traits. We are the composite of all of our traits and the degrees of each of our traits. And when we make changes in our life, the physical features on our faces also change. We are a dynamic process of evolving.

When we look at type casting, we can thank Hollywood for doing such a magnificent job of picking actors for specific roles. We would not expect Omar Sharif to play in the "Make my day" roles like Clint Eastwood. We could not see Scarlet O'Hara being played by Doris Day or John Candy playing an imprisoned Jew in the concentration camp in Schindler's List. We normally think of certain personalities as naturally fitting for certain roles.

In our own lives, however, we have a distinct advantage over these actors in their assigned scripts and roles. Although we are born with our innate gifts, talents and challenges (our personality), we are given a more precious gift- the gift of choice. As we consciously begin to redirect our automatic actions and reactions in areas of our lives where we have difficulties, we create better habits which lead to a new lifestyle. Our facial features (physical structure) actually change as we change our behavior (our function.)

These changes can be validated in our personality profile charts where traits are scientifically measured with instruments at different times of a person's life. When people make desired changes, their physical features can be scientifically measured for that change. It is gratifying to see this validation; that form and function are closely related and dependent upon each other. As we deliberately and consistently make changes in our life style habits, styles of acting, feeling, thinking, and our form (our facial features) changes also. All these changes are a reflection of our choices.

In our workshops, we invite participants to bring photos from different times in their lives, babyhood to present day. We know we would rarely look like our baby pictures. We can see physical changes throughout our lives—all showing how our choices have changed us physically.

In life, we are never faced with generalities. We are, however, always faced with the specifics. It isn't what is said to you, but how the personality of the person speaking delivers his words; how they affect you, with all your own personality filters. This is why knowing your own basic traits and how they function will contribute significantly to your ability to successfully choose ways to bring about mutually satisfying outcomes when you communicate daily with people- face to face.

Regardless of our race, our physical attributes give clues to those who know how to read them, of how we feel, think and will likely act. Even more important, they signal to others how we would like them to communicate with us. Knowing these road signs will make the journey of interacting with others much smoother, more interesting, more predictable and much more respectful of the other person's individuality.

As you look at each trait presented, remember to look for the scores that are high or low and where you fit in. If you cannot tell, you are likely in the middle range. You are more balanced than the extremely high or low scores.

You likely will find it challenging to relate to people with opposite scores. You may also wonder once in a while when it is "going to be your time," to be understood,   accepted and appreciated. That is both the challenge and the blessing of being a balanced score. As you read about the high and low scores on each trait, try to think of someone you know whose trait fits the description, or if you fit one of the descriptions. Then observe if the way they automatically act or think fits the individual trait.

The next step will be the combining of the traits and the intensity of each of them for one person's personality. There will be no one person like another person, since each trait score will differ. You will never be bored at parties, airports and will find the information helpful in dealing with people face to face.

As you read this book, you will begin to see how you are unique in your own individuality as are other people. You can then use this information in all aspects of your personal and professional life – anywhere you are dealing with people, face to face. This book gives you valuable tools to understand and easily connect with people you meet. You will be able to "know" the other person and choose interactions that will benefit both of you- *At First Glance.*

PART ONE
Facial Traits

Introduction to Facial Traits

It is our structure (especially our facial features) that inclines our current personality and gives us definite ways to predict how a person will respond automatically, according to their innate traits. Our face reveals how we think and react to events and people around us. As we grow and change, so too do our facial features. Few people look like their baby pictures. Our structure keeps changing throughout our lifetime.

We see how people with certain builds are best at different sports; how the movie directors have an uncanny sense of who will play what role best. Understanding certain traits enable us to find vocations that make us happy, enable us to establish rapport quickly, let us easily understand and accept other people's differences instead of judging them and feeling distanced by their behavior.

We all try to read people every day in personal and professional life; with varying degrees of success. It is easy, however, to "read the person" before they gesture, speak, give inflections, tones or glances if you use their structure.

To date, over 68 traits have been empirically and statistically verified and proven to be scientifically significant to the 1% level. Further, these traits have been organized according to the sections of the human where they occur naturally and range from 1-10 in scoring. We will look at several key physical characteristics (facial features) and learn what the trait means, how to recognize the scores of low or high and what to do when you see these extremes in an individual whose scorings are much different from yours.

Please note that if you cannot place yourself as either a low or high score, then you are likely in the middle range (a 4-6 score). Each trait is neither good nor bad; they simply have advantages and disadvantages depending upon the action in the moment. The middle-range trait people have an advantage over both extremes because they can relate to both scores and their challenge is wondering "when is it going to be my turn." They make good mediators, counselors, negotiators; anywhere a need for both sides to be heard and understood.

The science of reading people is called Personology, but a simpler approach is to understand people by reading their faces. Many of the key features are located on the face. This is why we suggest learning several of the most important traits you will see as you approach a person for the first time. You will be able to know and understand that person *very* well . . . . *At First Glance*

These personality traits are found mostly on the human head. For example, the **Thinking area** is naturally found around the forehead and governs how we process our information and the amount of capacity for thinking itself. The **Feeling and Emotion area** reflect how we react emotionally and are more likely to feel as we first experience things in our daily life and is a band through our eye areas and around our head. Surprisingly enough, there are a lot of traits located in this area. The **Action area** traits around the parietal of the head show how much energy we will exert in our immediate activities and our long range goals. The **Automatic Expression area** which does not have feeling or thinking involved are labeled "automatic" since they go into action without processing. These traits are located on the lower part of the face jaw, chin etc. The **Physical Trait** area relates to the physical structure itself and the current condition of the entire body.

All personality traits relate to us as *unique* individuals, and there is no way to make generalizations. These traits are not sex linked. In other words, they are categorized as neither male nor female. Further, the measuring for these traits may have a slightly different starting point in different races, but all scorings of traits are valid cross culturally. For example, our Asian friends may, as a race, have generally higher set eyebrows, and the starting point for lowest score may be different than our Caucasian friends, but within their race the same measuring scores of 1 to 10 are accurately presented.

I suggest that when you look in the mirror at your own traits, hold the mirror vertically straight and at your eye level. This will give you accuracy in determining your own scoring. When you first look at your traits, it is best to think in terms of how high or low you are with each trait, or are you in the middle range. When you begin looking at other people, try taking one trait a week. For one week, just look at eyebrows – and notice if they are high or low. Look for the extremes first to give you more confidence in reading faces. You will begin to notice how fascinating, different and unique each person is and you will see how easy it is for you to "get in step" with them or truly understand them in a very special real way.

Your understanding and appreciation of yourself and others will deepen as you study their faces on the outside and begin to know them on the inside. Your skills of communication, compassion, perception and your ability to find ways to connect with all those people in your life will be greatly enhanced when you truly can know them—*At First Glance.*

How to Use This Book
to Your Best Advantage

I suggest that you read through the book once, then:

1. Take one facial feature (trait) at a time. Look at yourself in the mirror. (When using a hand mirror, hold the mirror vertical to your face and look at your facial feature at eye level. Looking up or down, holding the mirror at an angle will not give you an accurate reading of your trait.)

2. Appreciate how you are configured presently. Know you are ever-changing and that since your childhood your features have had some changes. Any changes that you make in your daily habits of thinking and acting will create differences in your lifestyle, and then changes will occur in your physical face and body. Look at your baby pictures to present day and notice the changes.

3. Take that same trait for a week and begin to look at other people. Notice if that trait is different than yours –higher or lower in score (do they have more or less than your trait).

4. Add one more trait each week. As you begin to put the traits together, you will notice that some

traits augment (amplify) others and some traits may diminish how other traits influence our automatic
behavior.

5. As we make conscious choices to act differently, we redirect our habits into positive actions, create more harmonious successful experiences, live rewarding lifestyles, enrich our relationships and enjoy contentment with ourselves and others. When we make these changes, the physical features on our faces actually change and can be verifiably measured in a Personality Profile Chart. When we do in-depth profile charts, we use instruments to measure over 80 different traits on an individual. When clients return (after making some positive changes in habits) and we measure them again, they can scientifically see their changes besides knowing their changes internally.

This book covers a few of the basic traits you will want to use when meeting people for the first time and for connecting and communicating with all the people in your life.

Good Luck! Enjoy discovering your beautiful and unique self as well as understanding people in your personal and professional life.

1. DISCRIMINATIVE
Facial Trait

Timing of instinctive, emotional selectivity.
Physical Attribute: Distance of eyebrows above
the eye opening.

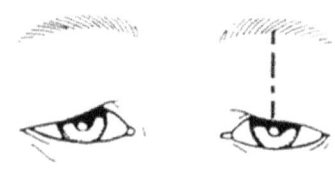

HIGH SCORE

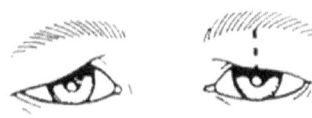

LOW SCORE

High score (8) eyebrows set high above the eyes and referred to as "high brow":

People who score high on discriminative are very selective about most everything in their life. Their
choices are on the feeling-emotion level and it takes
them time to make their selections. In new or unclear

situations, they appear reserved until they feel com-fortable. They instinctively create space to allow themselves time to get familiar with the situation and/or with you.

Do not take this seeming distancing personally. It is their natural approach to life. They feel violated and discounted if someone invades their personal space and makes assumptions without going "through channels" first or using what they consider proper protocol for the circum-stances.

For example, they would be completely turned off if, upon first meeting, someone violates these rules and treats them in a "casual" manner, move in quickly and stand too close to them. It feels like their person-al space has been rudely invaded.

If their first impression of you is that you were "up close and personal" with them before they felt com-fortable, it will be extremely difficult for you to get a second chance.

They may be seen by people with a low score on dis-criminative (affable) as being judgmental, haughty, cold, impersonal, "stuck up" and unfeeling. They are also perceived as appearing as though they are "ex-clusive."

Underneath this aloof look is a warm and feeling person whom you will have the opportunity to know when you allow them to unfold in their own time and way. They can be just as warm and friendly as those with a low brow once they are comfortable with you. If you wait for them to invite you into their "inner circle," they will be totally committed.

High brows (discriminative 8) by their nature, observe before they absorb.

Their theme phrase is: "Let me observe first, then respond or act."
Their helper phrase is: "I'll be more spontaneous initially."

Low score (2) Eyebrows are set low above eyes. Sometimes called a "Low Brow"-

People who score low on discriminative (affable), automatically and easily fit right into new situations. They are extremely casual about their approach in life. They move in quickly and get to know people right away because they have few filters that things have to go through before they accept them. They act like old friends.

They flow with things, find it easy to meet new people and naturally engage themselves in the conversations and the lives of others. It seems as no one is a stranger to these people. They can be in unfamiliar places and in a very short time create friendships with strangers. These friendships, however, will be more casual. People with low scores on discriminative automatically fit right into new situations that are casual. They can get to know people fast because they have fewer filters that they process through. They flow with things, quickly meet new people and engage themselves in conversations and the lives of others without having to think about it. They seem to adapt easily with whatever is going on.

Their warm, friendly and outgoing nature tends to draw people to them. It feels easy to approach people with low set eyebrows because they have ways of making you feel like you have known them for a long time and they treat you like a familiar friend.

For many people this is endearing and charming. It makes it easy to begin conversation, conduct business and quickly move through the introductory amenities.

Their casual, comfortable style uses no formalities or stuffy language. Their dress code, if they have one, includes the basic, simple and comfortable apparel. They will probably only wear ties and suits upon demand, preferring casual clothing, soft-soled shoes or resort wear.

On first meeting, they appreciate people who sit closer, talk in direct simple personal ways, call them by their first name or nickname immediately, and touching them is fine.

Their theme phrase is: "Come on in. I'll decide later if we fit together."

Their helper phrase is: "Let me thoughtfully choose first, then invite those who fit well."

If the other person has less of this trait than you (their eyebrows are set low above their eyes and yours are set high above your eyes:

Dress in comfortable clothes that are more casual. If you overdress when meeting them, they will feel uncomfortable. If you happen to meet them and you are "over-dressed," you could take your suit jacket off and loosen or remove your tie, for example.

Be the first to reach out and shake hands in a friendly and casual way. Touching their forearm when shaking their hand is reassuring.

You can sit or stand closer than is probably comfortable for you so they can feel you like them. They will feel fine if they are sitting and you pull up a chair close to sit down and talk with them.

You can call them by their first name, using familiar and warm tones in your voice. Be direct with them. Avoid anything that would make your interaction with them stuffy or a ritual.

Plan on meeting at places that have a more casual environment. If planning an activity, choose one that by its nature lends itself towards a comfortable and casual experience.

Appreciate their quick interest in you or your product. You may think they are completely sold on you, but do not take their familiarity and genuine easygoing manner as a real commitment. In their mind, their engaging manner means only that they are interested.
If they do say "yes", it means that it is true for them at the present time. They know they can always change their minds later after they think about it.

Their flavorful, friendly personality at first meeting will give you the impression they are definitely interested in you – which may translate as a real commitment in your mind. However, as easy as it is for them to involve themselves with you, it is just as easy for them to change their minds.

If something is important to you, be sure to double check on agreements with them to make sure you are both still on the same wave length as they may change their minds.

The intent of both scores is to appropriately assess new information about something in order to become involved or to accept people.

High scores process many distinctions before choosing to become involved with other people.

Low scores make few distinctions before becoming involved and make their choices afterwards.

2. ANALYTICAL

Facial Trait

The need to process (analyze) things before acting in any situation. This process operates from a feeling level and the higher the score, the longer the timing of response before going into action.

Physical attribute: The amount of epicanthic fold (skin) covering the upper eyelid; the more the eyelid is covered, the higher the score.

HIGH SCORE

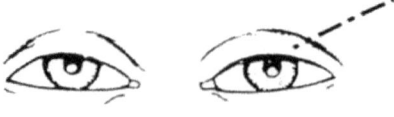

LOW SCORE

High score (8): eyelids completely covered:

People with high scores on analytical are constantly making comparisons on a feeling emotional level.

They feel a great need to consider, compare and study all the parts of something before taking action. They often tend to overanalyze information that they already have processed.

Their main focus is to "look at" enough of the pieces so they get a good sense of the whole picture before they decide to buy or become involved in a person or project.

They have a strong need to know the reasons behind things, to be aware of the other person's motives and to understand the steps involved before coming to a conclusion and taking action. When asked to do something, they have to know "why" first, and then have to have time to "consider" it.

It takes time to process these many pieces of information before they can comfortably make decisions or give commitments. If they do not get these pieces of information or if they aren't given enough time to think about it beforehand, they feel extreme pressure and appear resistant, stubborn, slow thinking or in-decisive.

Other people may experience them as being obstructive, slowing down their progress or blocking them from what they want to do. In addition, since this "analytical process" slows down the response time, they may be seen as getting stuck in the minor details and not able to move into action.

Highly analytical people may continue to analyze the same things they have already processed. They tend to be more receptive to new ideas when they are not thrown unexpectedly into situations and not given enough preparation time to process the information about the situation or the change.

If preliminary facts are presented leading up to the main point, and the "why" of things are revealed along with the facts or request, they are more able to move along towards making a decision and not spending so much time mulling things over and over.

Highly analytical people could benefit from learning to respond more spontaneously in the daily minor things of life or answer questions more quickly and by not reading more into the situation or not questioning what someone says is really there.

They could practice making decisions on small matters more quickly and leaving their analyzing skills for the major matters in life.

They benefit themselves and those around them by learning to live in a more spontaneous manner.

Their theme phrase is: "Let's think it through thoroughly first and maybe mull it over again."

Their helper phrase is: "I have enough information. Let's act now!"

Low score Analytical (2): very little skin folded over the eyelid.

These people are much more action oriented. They tend to go into action without analysis. They are much more comfortable with the basic information and getting to the bottom line so they can act.

They are the doers; they want to move into action as quickly as possible. They feel a need to cut through the emotional red tape and get to the final results. They quickly feel bogged down with so much analyzing and become impatient and restless if pushed to consider too many of the parts in the process of decisions. They do not like to sit and process; they like to understand the key points and then move into action.

They will become impatient and turned off when working with people who insist on knowing all the details of who, what, when, where, why, how and now... "Let's rethink things again."

Because they are much more interested in summarizing the basic points and going into action, they may appear ruthless or inconsiderate to others who need to think things through in detail before they can act.

Other people may see them as more interested in getting the job done, than considering their feelings as human beings.

Direct action people are just as warm and sensitive as other people, but they are focused on the end result, not all the steps in between.

Their drive to see a project to completion makes them unaware or uninterested in all the steps in between. They like it when they're given the key points first, then a few statements about what needs to be done, a quick summary; then action!

Because they are such action-oriented people, they are usually involved in more projects than they can handle. Sometimes they find themselves waist high in quicksand before they take time to puzzle about, "How did I get here?"

Their theme phrase is: "Let's do it now."
Their helper phrase is: "Think this through twice before going into action."

If the other person is more analytical than you, (you are more direct action oriented):

Expect them to take much longer to make decisions or process information since they will -have lots of questions and need answers before feeling comfortable about deciding or acting on decisions.

Acknowledge their need to analyze much of what you are saying and encourage them to ask questions to help things become clear to them. They will have lots of questions before feeling comfortable about deciding what   action is best for them.

Remember this "analyzing" is on a feeling emotional level so it may not make "logical" sense, although they will believe it does.

Be patient and set aside more time than you would normally allow. Be prepared to explain everything. Let them know that you are there to help answer any and all questions that they may have. Explain fully the reasons behind your statements until they are satisfied. Gaps or inconsistencies will be noted, resulting in resistance and confusion that will slow you down even more. Be patient.

Help them evaluate information to get to the big picture quicker and cover some of the pieces of information as they cannot see the whole picture. They are much more interested in the process of the parts. Understand that even when they get the picture, they may still have to "mull it over" again to see how things fit. Allow extra time for this; even set a follow up time to review things.

Remember they have a great skill of figuring things out if given enough time.

Reason with them, explain your facts, talk slowly and lead up to your main points carefully showing how each part is linked to the next part. If you do not, you will lose them.

Be patient and slow down your own desire to move ahead quickly. Move along at their pace and they will feel you understand them better.

If you need to, set an additional time to meet to give them time to think things through on their own. This will help you not to become frustrated or impatient. Set another appointment date soon enough while with them so they don't forget you or over analyze so much they decide against you.

If it is too short, they won't have time to review in their own minds; if it is too long, they may over-analyze themselves against the idea you have proposed.

Remember if you do not cover enough of the parts of your information, they cannot see it and will auto-matically   resist what you are proposing.

If the other person is less analytical than you, (they are a more direct action person):

Get to the key points fast and first. Next, explain what facts support your points. Don't overload them with many details or lengthy explanations. You will only appear irritating, plodding, a slow thinker, dragging things out and they will lose interest in what you are saying. Only give them enough explanation to get your points across, and then move on.

Make your communication feel active to them by showing them what results are readily possible. Do not get them involved in the process of getting there. You can expect them to be ready to take action quickly.

Do not give long descriptive explanations of the reasons why things are, the reasoning behind your thoughts or the causes of things unless they specifically ask about them. Just make succinct statements. If they need further information, they will ask you for it.

Try and appreciate their ability to cut through red tape and get things done. Do not take personally their brusque manner and laser focus on end results. They are doing their best to get to the perceived goal. If you have to cover some steps in between, quickly show them how they relate directly to the end result; then move along. Don't drag out your communication. You will create rapport quickly with them when you acknowledge interest in getting results fast and support their need to move things along.

Remember, they are basically "doers" not "thinkers." Everything you can do to help them know there is movement in the moment will help them relax and feel that progress is being made.

You could mention that your tendency is to examine all the parts and make sure everything is covered in depth; but ask them to interrupt you if you get off on a tangent as you also wish to collaboratively get to the bottom line and go into proper action.

Assure them you are not just "talking words." Give them a sense their time is well spent, and you understand their needs to feel things are moving along. **Inner intent of both high score and low score is to analyze situations to make the best decisions and take action.**

High scores feel a need to analyze all the parts before deciding to take action.

Low scores want only the main points and need to quickly go into action.

3. EMOTIONAL EXPRESSIVENESS
Facial Trait

Visible amount of emotion expressed in the moment.

Physical Attribute: size of the iris compared to the white portion of the eye. The larger the iris (more of the colored part of the eye), the higher the score.

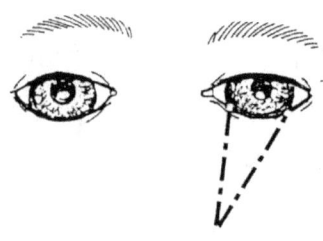

HIGH SCORE

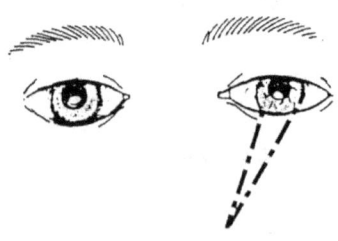

LOW SCORE

High score (8) a high degree of colored part of eye (iris) showing as compared to the white part of the eye:

People who have large irises are automatically overly expressive of their feelings. They laugh easily, they cry easily. Whatever emotion they are feeling, they instantly express it. Because they are so in touch with their feelings, their moods tend to change frequently.

Because their feelings are so close to the surface, they are expressed as soon as they feel them. They will likely appear warm, affectionate, demonstrative, compassionate and caring when they feel accepted. They are very sentimental and tend to "wear their hearts on their sleeves."

When they are ignored, they take it personally and get their feelings hurt very easily. They perceive it as being rejected and judged. They then react with self-pity. If they sense any slights or indications of disinterest in them personally, they take it as signs that they are not appreciated or loved. They need constant reassurances from others that they are loved.

Since highly emotional people are more interested in feelings than proper action, they tend to excuse themselves and other loved ones rather than taking right and responsible action. They could benefit by focusing on what the correct action for the situation should be rather than how they feel. It helps them to consider how to act, not react.

Traditionally, men in our western society have been trained to hold in their feelings by being told "Act manly," or "Big boys don't cry." Consequently, it is common to find men with smaller irises than women since it is acceptable for women to cry. However, this is different in Latin American and Eastern cultures where the outward expression of emotion is acceptable behavior for men.

People with large irises most often will make decisions from their feelings and not their logical reasoning.

This is important to note when they are making commitments to you as their feelings may change quickly. Therefore, it is easier for a highly emotional person to justify his or her change of heart.

Low score: (2) very little colored iris showing in eyes and lots of white of eye showing:

People with very little iris showing in their eye and lots of white tend to withhold (suppress) expressing their emotions. They still have strong feelings, but those feeling are held deep inside of them. They appear to control their emotions much easier, and are less demonstrative of what they feel.

They do not feel comfortable when others exhibit outbursts of emotions. They are not known for shedding tears or spontaneously displaying any other emotions.

Their self-contained appearance may give others the impression that they don't care or they are unfeeling. In reality, they feel that an external outpouring of emotions is inappropriate.

They prefer to handle problems logically and use their clear thinking processes. This makes it comfortable for them to handle situations and people in a more objective manner.

They are able to cut through emotional baggage and take needed action in stressful situations because they are making decisions from their head and not their heart.

Low score emotional expressive people look towards the performance expected instead of making excuses for others or themselves. They may appear unfeeling, cold, indifferent and uncaring to others. In close relationships, this feeling about them is even more amplified.

People with a low score of emotional expressiveness could benefit from listening to what the other person is feeling rather than demanding immediate action.

They could further benefit by consciously cultivating a softer tone of their voice and by showing genuine interest in how the other person feels.

They can help a relationship by trying to sense how the other person feels. They can enrich relationships with those they love by listening without giving advice as most often highly emotional expressive people just want to be heard and feel someone cares. It would also be good for less expressive people to share some of their own feelings, too without feeling that people are prying.

If the other person has more of this trait than you, (they have large irises and you have smaller irises):

Be more emotionally responsive to them. Express your thoughts in a warm and caring tone. Smile. Be more demonstrative of your positive feelings. You may feel like you are being overly dramatic, but if you have a caring tone, the person will greatly appreciate it.

Do not react negatively to their emotional roller coaster or their emotional outbursts. Rather let them feel your concern about their hurt.

Show a genuine and personal interest in the person. Be more sympathetic. Do things that will make the person feel you personally care for him or her. An invitation to a genuine congenial lunch will go a long way to make this person feel special.

Ask about their family members and friends you both know. Send thank you notes, remember their birthday, make personal calls, keep in touch with them, etc. All of these acts tell the person how important he/she is to you. Your tender, gentle feelings and respectful caring is what is wanted and needed and will be cherished.

If the other person has less of this trait than you, (they have small irises and you have large irises):

Speak in a more logical and businesslike manner. Do not show or share your emotions as this will create an uncomfortable and awkward situation for them and you.

Remember that this person has strong feelings deep down inside of them that you are not privileged to know about. Be respectful of their need for emotional privacy.

Control your instinctive response to react emotionally to what is being said or done. They do not relate to displays of emotions and will withdraw, become angry and appear cold. In their minds, you have over-stepped your boundaries. Focus instead on the information you are giving them. Present your facts efficiently, properly, courteously with a more matter of fact attitude.

Do not let your personal feelings spill over into the conversation. Avoid asking them personal questions.

Do not bring up your personal stories and problems as they will not likely be sympathetic. Remember they are interested in performance, not popularity.

Inner intent of both the high and low emotional expressiveness is to express emotions appropriately.

High scores do it by expressing whatever they are feeling in the moment.

Low scores do it by expressing thoughts instead and suppressing their feelings.

4. TOLERANCE

Facial Trait

Basic timing of emotional reaction to what
is seen or heard.

Physical Attribute: Amount of space between the eyes
(inner canthi); the greater the space, the more emotional tolerance the person has. The less amount of
space the less tolerance the person has. An important
trait as it governs how a person perceives everything.

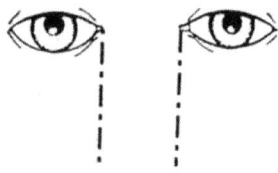

HIGH SCORE

LOW SCORE

High Score (8); high tolerance: eyes widely spaced.

People with widely spaced eyes are easy going, see events as far in the distance, don't notice details needing attention, overlook people's flaws, inconsistencies and behavior for a long time before dealing with them; appear broadminded, relaxed, and adaptable; forgive and forget.

They're seen as lackadaisical, procrastinators, inefficient with time and resources; late for appointments, project completions; sometimes noncommittal in relationships.

Low score (2) Low Tolerance: eyes close-set.

People with close-set eyes (less than one eye aperture apart,) see specifically, focus in the present moment, notice small flaws, potential problems and feel an urgency to fix them.

They perform precision work with deadlines well, are very reliable, value high ethical standards and demand others do the same.

Unfortunately, the world often doesn't meet their expectations and they quickly become upset, irritated, frustrated, intolerant and inflexible at unfulfilled agreements, deadlines, and missed appointments.

If the other person has more of this trait than you (they have lots of space between eyes and you have very little space):

Expect a relaxed attitude and slower reaction time. Help them with prioritizing and details to keep on schedule.

Check each step of task to stay focused.

Reconfirm appointments; give friendly reminders on timelines. Appreciate that they'll forgive your mishaps.

If the other person has less of this trait than you (they have close set eyes and you have wide spaced eyes):

Do everything "exactly right," thoroughly, accurately and timely.

Keep promises or they'll feel lack of respect, integrity, commitment.

Perform, don't talk; act immediately; they want it now!
Prepare well; they'll quickly notice lapses, inefficiencies, and incompetency.

Intent of both is to properly respond (emotionally) to what is seen or heard.

High scores – take longer to respond and act.

Low scores - take very little time to respond and act.

5. SELF-CONFIDENCE

Facial Trait

A feeling of adequacy in new situations.

Physical Attribute: broadness of face (measured through eye sockets and the turn of forehead to chin)

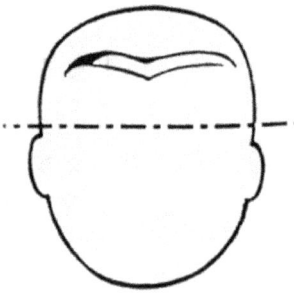

HIGH SCORE

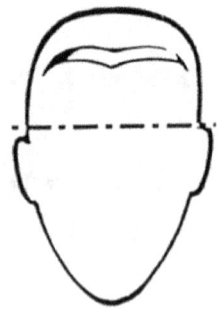

LOW SCORE

High score (8) broad shield face, wide through eye sockets:

Broad shield-faced people instinctively feel comfortable assuming responsibility without a lot of experience or preparation. In new situations, they easily take charge. When first exposed to a threat, new incident or challenge they instinctively feel that no matter what happens they can handle it. They instantly assume responsibility and do not back down in confronted situations. They feel quite adequate being in charge and many times do so without even being asked to become a leader.

Although they appear overpowering to many, they feel that if they don't take charge of the task at hand, it may not get done at all. However, it is much more difficult for them to take orders and follow directions from other people.

Since these innately self-confident people look so capable, others tend to look to them for leadership and answers. Subsequently, they inspire many people with their confident manners.

They tend to dismiss minor problems and feel they will handle whatever has to be taken care of as it comes along. They appear very courageous and are usually very thorough in the way they act and speak. They see things in a big picture manner and don't get bogged down with details.

They tend to challenge other people easily and possibly do not respect more reticent yet capable leaders by giving them an opportunity to share in the lead. They respect people who act confident and reassured. Their bold take-charge attitude is often intimidating.

Their Achilles heel is that when they do come up against something they cannot handle, it is emotionally devastating to them. They are stunned and overwhelmed at this rare experience.

Their theme phrase is: "I'm here; of course I can do it. Here's what you need to do."
Their helper phrase is: "Let me be supportive of others' abilities too."

Low score (2): long narrow face

Instinctively feels their own limitations when presented with new situations; needs preparation ahead of time.

Physical attribute: extremely long narrow face when compared to width of face through the eyes.

A long narrow faced person instinctively feels hesitant when presented with new situations. They feel they cannot adequately deal with it without preparing ahead of time.

They hesitate to begin acting without support or having time to prepare ahead of time for the task at hand. They feel vulnerable when they come up against people, information or things they do not know or understand.

Longer, narrow faced people have to do a lot of mental preparation to be able to handle many things in life. Their confidence is an "earned" confidence rather than innate confidence. They systematically learn piece by piece the new skills that allow them to feel confident in certain situations and become an expert in an area.

For them, it takes a lot of courage to risk and take charge of situations. Most people do not realize how much effort they require to do something new.

It is extremely devastating for them to be demeaned or belittled especially in public. They need support for each thing they accomplish and encouragement to try the next step. In work situations, it is best for them to have a segment of a project to work on rather than being given the entire project all at once. They are very good learners because they are willing to listen and learn from others without feeling that they already know it all.

They work well in supportive roles and are more than willing to let the other person be in the limelight and in charge. Responsibility is an extraordinarily important role for them and they take it very seriously.

Throughout history we have seen fine leaders and some of them with low scores on innate self-confidence. They have been successful by carefully preparing for such roles and by placing support systems beneath them.

Their theme phrase: "I'll need a lot of preparation before I can act."
Their helper phrase: "Let me begin acting now and prepare as I go along."

If the other person has more of this trait of confidence than you (they have a broad

shield face and you have a long narrow face,)

Speak to them in a tone that is definite and confident of what you are saying. Speak as though you know well what you are speaking about. Put your thoughts into more global perspectives; this will stretch your comfort zone. They will feel more comfortable working with you.

Focus on the big picture, not all the details. You will gain their attention and respect fast if you can think, act and talk in big terms.

Prepare well ahead to confront any of their objections directly and openly. Do not allow yourself to be intimidated thus, shrinking yourself. They will see this type of behavior as wishy-washy and indecisive, just the opposite of what you want to convey. As you must rehearse your confident presentation, do it well in advance so it will feel natural as you talk to them.

Begin by recalling a time when you felt absolutely invincible. This will help you feel and act more self-contained as you deal with them.

Anticipate that they will challenge you. Do not let their questioning make you feel they don't think you know your subject. They will feel your response (which should be in a most confident manner) will clearly state that you do know what you are talking about.

You will indeed be matching their own style that they are comfortable with—that being confident in self.

If the other person has less of this trait than you (they have a long narrow face and you have a broad shield face):

Tone down your expressions. Your voice should become quieter, the tone of your voice needs to soften and the way you speak should be gentle and non-threatening.

When you gesture, make your movements smooth, not large and dynamic. It is important that you become more sensitive and realize that other people are much more self-conscious of themselves than you. They will take any slight or indication that they are being criticized to heart and lose face. Always keep in mind that they are easily embarrassed. It is important to give them reassurance of your support, under-standing and approval.

Do not interrupt them when they are speaking. They interpret this as meaning you do not respect them or think what they have to say is important. Patiently listen to what they have to say without remarks.

Since they are self-conscious by nature, when they (occasionally) ask for your feedback, praise something you like before suggesting any changes. Acknowledge what it took for them to accomplish what has been done thus far.

Let them know you support and respect their feelings and ideas. Be delicate when you make your com-ments for changes.

Do not be confrontational or make them feel that they are under any scrutiny. Reaffirm your appreciation of them as a person at the end.

Approach them with your suggestions in a gentle, in-formative, collaborative way and cover only a small amount of specific information each time. This will allow them to realistically fix what has to be done.

Don't overwhelm them with requests, as they will lose confidence.

Resist your impulse to tell them how and what they should do. Give up the need to be in charge and remind yourself that there may be other people more qualified to lead than you. Ask yourself what you can do to learn from this person in this situation, rather than what you can teach them.

Intention of both is to feel adequate acting in new situations.

High scores feel confident acting without preparation in new situations.

Low scores feel adequate acting only after much preparation for new situations.

6. SELF-RELIANCE

Facial Trait

A basic reliance upon self.

Physical attribute: flared nostrils.
The more flared, the higher the score.

HIGH SCORE

LOW SCORE

High score (8) wide flared nostrils:

People with wide flared nostrils find it very important to make their own decisions. It is natural for them to turn to themselves instead of others since they instinctively feel that they know themselves better than anyone else.

Even if another person is an authority on an aspect of information they are interested in, they still feel that they ultimately know themselves best and will make the best decisions for themselves. They resist letting anyone else tell them what to do.

High score self-reliant people act as their own authority and move freely into situations they feel they can handle—in their own way. They tend to do things on their own and like to figure things out for themselves. They rely upon their past experiences and own feelings to tell them what to do in new situations.

These people find it easier to be in business for themselves so they can do things their own way.

Difficulties arise in working situations if specific instructions are not given to these workers since they will go ahead and do things their own way, not because they are consciously sabotaging the project, but they are simply following their own instincts. It is best if they work under a supervisor, that they are given a portion of work that has to be done, and a time to complete it and leave it up to them on how they will accomplish it. This allows them some freedom to "do it their own way."

Their theme phrase is: "My way, I'll do it my way." Their helper phrase is: "I see your way has merit too."

Low score (2) narrow nostrils (no flare):

People with a low score on self-reliance rely upon other people for their advice, opinions and reassurances. They are more apt to give up their own authority when they think that someone else may have better information. They tend to not only look toward outside sources for information, but also check many other sources before making their decisions.

They are able to learn new things better because they are willing to suspend their own ideas of how things are or should be. They are willing to follow instructions and take orders since they do not have resistance about being in charge and having things their own way. They look to others for approval before taking action on new projects, decision, purchases, etc.

Their theme phrase is: "Help me find my way."
Their helper phrase is: "I can think things through on my own before checking outside sources."

If the other person has more of this trait than you (they have flared nostrils and you have narrow or no nostrils):

They will naturally want to make their own decisions and feel that they are in charge of themselves and whatever activity you are involved with them. Let them do things their way, if possible.

Ask for their opinions if you can when giving them information so they feel they are in control of part of the process.

Ask for their advice on how to best accomplish what you both have set out to do together. Make it easy for them to join in the process by exploring their opinions and wherever possible include their ideas and suggestions.

Most babies are born with flared nostrils, and as children are growing up, it is a natural help for children to become more independent about basic life skills.

Their young theme song in the early formative years is "My Way." Later in life, those with high scores on self-reliance tend to continue to sing that song and use this phrase: "Always question authority and think for yourself."

If the other person has less of this trait than you (your nostrils are flared and theirs are not flared):

Be prepared to give them advice since they will ask your opinion as they are unsure of their own authority and hesitate to take action on their own. Your suggestions will likely be appreciated.

 Allow them more time to make their final decisions because they will need to check a number of sources before coming to their conclusion.

When you have given a task or project to a person with a lower score on self-reliance, remember to let them also have the authority to get the job or task done. Your instinctive reaction will be to take it back and do it yourself. Resist this temptation. Other people need to learn how to handle things on their own and you need to let go of the need to be in control. When delegating a responsibility, also give genuine authority.

Help people with a low score on self-reliance to learn to depend more upon themselves. Ask them gentle questions that help them probe more into their own thoughts, opinions and desires. Let them feel that you value their thoughts also. In addition and more important is that you encourage them to value their own internal wisdom above all others.

Move more slowly when pressing them for decisions and allow them processing time to compare notes with other information they will have obtained from other sources. Motivate them not to blindly accept what the authorities in the field have to say over their own inner sense of what is best for them.

Support how they feel, think and act regardless of your own opinion. Encourage them to take responsibility for themselves, before relying upon outside "authorities."

The inner intent of both is to rely upon a proper authority to make decisions.

High scores instinctively rely upon an inside source (themselves) when making decisions.

Low scores tend to rely upon outside sources (others) before making decisions.

7. VERBAL STYLE

Facial Trait

Style of verbal expression (oral or written)

Physical attribute: Thickness or thinness of the upper lip as compared to the overall size of the face. The thicker the upper lip, the higher the score on verbal style.

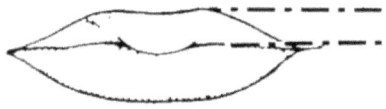

HIGH SCORE

LOW SCORE

High score (8) thick upper lip:

People with thick upper lips are very wordy. They express themselves easily and fully in speech and in writing. As they open their mouths to speak, their thoughts then begin to form and you are included in the process.

You will have the rich experience of being with them fully as they speak to you. You hear in their words a complete verbal picture. They stop thinking as they close their lips.

Those with high verbal scores will reply to your simple question using many words, adjectives and paragraphs instead of a one-sentence answer.

They may use multiple adjectives, colorful words and tend to give you their full-unabridged version of their story.

They can talk for long periods even on subjects in which they are not particularly interested. Because of their volume of words, there may be few words that actually have relevant meaning.

They feel a need to take plenty of time to get their point across. They tend to be repetitive, elaborating on their thoughts as they go along. Their listeners may tire of waiting for them to get to the point or finish talking. They appear to others as rambling without direction.

Many times, listeners stop listening or become irritated with them since it takes so long to get to their point.

To the opposite type, the low verbal style (thin lipped) person, verbose people appear insincere, not forthright and not open. They are, of course, sincere, but their message tends to get lost in all the words floating around.

People often stop taking what they have to say as meaningful or authentic because of their profuse verbiage.

People with high scores form their verbal thoughts and verbal expression simultaneously. Therefore, they often lose their thought when they are interrupted in the middle of a sentence since they were in the middle of their thought.

Imagine the "high verbal style" person as one who sits down to write a nice long letter by hand to someone they haven't seen in a very long time. Because it will be a long letter, they will not be able to gather all their thoughts together in the beginning, and because it is written by hand, they will not be able to write it in a short time. It is a leisurely experience. They will want to share it completely with you, from the beginning thought to the end.

They incorporate into their communications, images and colorful feelings as they tell their story. In their mind, using more words and describing things more completely will give you the fullest experience possible.

They feel they are being effective with their words and are not concerned with efficiency. In addition, they also feel they are making their story more interesting for you by giving you more words, adjectives, etc.

On the other hand, people who score low verbal style (thin upper lips) cannot handle all their lengthy stories, the time it takes to listen to them and the many ways they tend to repeat the same thing.

Those with low verbal style like to have a simple, bare bones version. They like the old-fashioned western union telegram or a very brief email.

Often, those with high score of verbal complain that their mates don't listen to them. Most often, it is the length of time and the amount of words that need to be adjusted.

Their theme phrase is: "Let's just start talking. I want you to know all that led up to my conclusion before I give you the conclusion. Here is my complete story."

Their helper phrase is: "Let me think this out before I open my mouth. I'll give you my bottom line point of view or brief story and then you can ask me if you need more information."

Low score (2) thin upper lip:

People with a thin upper lip are very concise in their speech or writing. They tend to think about what to say, open their mouths and say it in as few words and little time as possible. They not only express themselves briefly, but also are more specific about what they say.

To people with high verbal scores, they appear as not caring to share their thoughts and feelings. However, low verbal scores feel uncomfortable with flowery language, long explanations and paragraphs.

Their style of expression is to streamline their sentences. Often their sentences include a verb, subject and an object. Rarely do you hear them use long phrases, dependent clauses and adjectives.

They automatically have their thoughts lined up before they open their mouths to speak. They do well with precise and clear directions and orders. They need only the essentials. Rarely do they "waste time" just talking. If they are interested in a subject or feel the need to talk, they may talk at length, but their sentence structure will be austere and simple. They will come to their point quickly and move on. They tend to cover a lot of ground in their communications because they don't mince words.

What you will experience from their communication is a quick snapshot of the finished painting. You will not know much about their journey and the steps in between of how they got to their bottom line, but you will be getting the bare bones edition – the final edition.

They respond quickly and finish what they have to say. You may get enough to understand what they are saying, but the way they respond is often misunderstood. They frequently appear as being too abrupt, curt, and dismissive. High verbal style individuals interpret their responses as disinterest or disliking them personally.

Where the low verbal style person feels they are being efficient with their words, they appear to others often as being ineffective. Their brief style leaves others feeling gypped of their experience and feeling unimportant. What they may hear are terse sounding short words and sounds that come out piercingly. The tone of the vowels is hard and there is no way to experience the feeling of their words in such brevity. Inside of the low score verbal person, they feel the words they say, but their listeners' ears cannot hear their feelings. Their inner feelings just do not come across and it causes many misunderstandings in relationships.

Low score verbal individual's challenge is to allow what they want to say (a thought, a thing, a feeling) to become more personalized and expanded in the communication; add more color, details, descriptions and cultivate a friendlier tone of voice and speak in smooth softer and rounder sounds. It may feel like they are overdramatizing it at first, but people need to feel more of what they feel.

Their theme phrase is: "Let me give you the bottom line thought."
Their helper phrase is: "Let me give you more description, adjectives, information."

If the other person is more verbal than you are, (they have a thick upper lip and you have a thin upper lip):

Do not interrupt them in the middle of a sentence; they will lose their train of thought. Ask very specific questions that require only brief responses. Do not ask open-ended questions or too general a question as they will tend to go off on tangents. Use words that narrow down their responses. Don't cut them short, as it will give them the impression you are not interested in them.

When you are responding to their questions, be as expansive as possible in your answers. Use more adjectives and details. Try to use a warm tone of voice.

For example, don't just tell them they look nice; describe in detail what about them looks so nice to you. Be patient with their need to explain things in detail and repeat things. They need to satisfy their need to fully express themselves.

They feel they are being effective with many words; you may feel they are being inefficient with many words.

You will have to keep them on track and help them get to their point. Set some definite guidelines for how long you will be able to meet. Also, ask them prior to getting together, to write down the main points they wish to talk to you about. You can remind them of these points during your time together.

In a social setting, early in the conversation, mention when you have to leave so it doesn't come as a shock to them when you do get ready to leave.

Express your appreciation of their earnest desire to have you understand them. If you are too brief in your responses, your motives may be suspect.

If the other person is lower on this trait of verbal style than you are, (they have a thin upper lip and you have a thick upper lip):

Remember thin-lipped people are very concise in their responses and expressions. Get to the point quickly and as briefly. You may need to write down an outline of what you'll cover.

When presenting your ideas, use as few words as possible. If you speak in "outline form", you may feel you are being rude, curt or uninterested.

Avoid talking excessively. Remember these people approve of verbal efficiency. Less is more. Do not repeat any information you have already given them unless they ask for it; as they will believe that you think they haven't been paying attention.

They feel it is a waste of time and energy to keep repeating "the same thing over and over again." Accept the challenge to think of what you want to say first and then speak, making every word count.

Use sentences that are short, clear, pertinent and un-cluttered. If you open your mouth and start talking non-stop, you will lose them entirely.

If you are having trouble keeping your statements brief, tell yourself that you cannot talk until you have drafted a mental telegram for this person. Imagine how concise you'd become if you paid $100 for every word you used in a telegram. You may be amazed how quickly you can find the essential words to use.

A helpful suggestions might be to just use a verb, subject and if needed, an object. They will feel you're moving the conversation along, not talking down to them and they will appreciate you for it.

Inner intent of both is to appropriately express thoughts.

High scores do it as they speak with more words.

Low scores form thoughts first; then speak with few words.

8. PHYSICAL INSULATION

Facial Trait

Timing of response to outside stimulus.

Physical Attribute: The thickness of the first layer of skin (epidermis.) The thicker the layer, the higher the score on physical insulation.

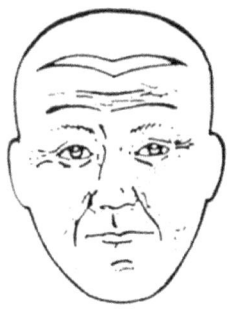

HIGH SCORE

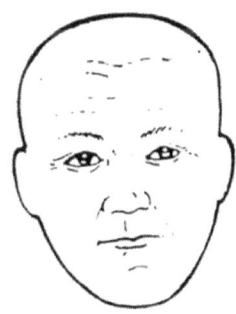

LOW SCORE

High score (8): thick first outer layer of skin.

Thickly insulated people have an outer layer of skin that has a coarse texture, larger pores, ruddier complexion and deeper lines. This is easily seen on the forehead. The epidermis is the first layer of skin that separates the sense perception nerve endings from the outer environment. The thicker the skin, the longer it will take for the person to respond. High scores usually have hair follicles that are coarser and denser.

People with a high score on physical insulation are well protected environmentally and emotionally. As their skin texture is more coarse and thick, it takes more of everything to reach them and longer time to reach them. They therefore process things slowly.

They are not as sensitive to everything in their environment. They do not feel the cold or heat as much. They are not easily bothered by sounds, smells, intense visual input or a hardy touch. All sensory input needs to be greater to reach them in a way that makes sense to them.

Basically, these people are a "more of" type. They usually appreciate heartier aromas, spicier foods, denser smells and greater volume of the sounds to which they are listening. If these sounds are music, the quality of the tone will probably have more bass tones and be more amplified. If it is in a conversation, they will appreciate someone speaking up, looking more directly at them, and perhaps even touching them with a firmer touch or handshake. The tone of their voice will also reflect the hardiness of what feels comfortable for them.

The texture of fabrics they choose will likely have a coarser fiber, and their colors will be bolder or earthier.

On an emotional level, the thicker insulated people are much less bothered by what others say or do simply because it takes more of everything to get to them. They do not personalize comments as quickly. Things seem to "roll off their backs" or go unnoticed.

They may appear to others as if they do not care or are not willing to take action on things that seem to bother others sooner. Once they become aware (the nerve receptor has been stimulated, the message has reached the brain and they have become aware of the problem) they may act quickly or not (depending upon other personality traits). High scores tend to prefer more quantity and are not as particular about quality.

Their theme phrase is: "I can handle more of everything without it bothering me. More is better."
Their helper phrase is: "I can become more sensitive and appreciate quality in things and people rather and wanting more stimuli. Less may be better."

Low score (2) thin first layer of skin:

People with a thin first layer of skin are more sensitive physically and emotionally. Their outer layer of skin is thinner, smooth, porcelain like, and silky in texture. If they have lines in their face and forehead, they will be finer and not too deep. The pores in their skin will not be easily visible. Their hair texture will be thinner and finer.

Because the skin layer which insulates them from the outside world is very thin, they feel things more quickly and more intensely. Their responses to whatever is happening in their environment (physically and emotionally) are quick and it takes very little to trigger their responses.

Since it takes "less of everything" to reach them, they are affected easily by changes in temperature, tastes, sounds, textures, smells.) They generally prefer a quieter environment with more refinement in their surroundings.

Their choice of clothing is for smoother fabrics and garments that will protect them from the weather, hot or cold. They appreciate a softer touch, quieter sounds, subtler aromas, gentler spices on their foods. They like quality rather than quantity. A little bit does go a long way with them. They do not care for raucous laughter, coarse jokes and crude behavior.

In a close relationship, this trait is magnified greatly, even with just a one-point difference in the scoring; as we are talking about skin tissue that covers from the top of the head to the tip of the toes.

Personal hygiene, for example, is more important to a thin-skinned person since they will notice body odors more quickly and may become bothered by the smells. For the thinly insulated person even a robust handshake can feel more like their hand is being crushed instead of clasped.

As they are finely attuned to changes in their sur-
rounds, they will notice changes in tones of voices
and may tend to personalize these as "lapses of refinement" by others. They benefit by putting a layer of
"mental insulation" around themselves in sensitive
situations so they do not as easily react to the words
and actions of more thickly insulated people.

Their theme phrase is: "Less is more. Give me quality
and not quantity."

Their helper phrase is: "Let me plan ahead for my
comforts (physical and mental) so I do not personalize
discomforts when with others."

**If the other person has more of this trait
than you do: they have a thicker first layer
of skin and you have a thinner first layer
of skin:**

Know that their style of expression, tastes and physical appearance will be more rugged than you would
prefer for your comfort zone. Do not take their robust
appearance and perhaps unrefined mannerisms as a
direct reflection on how they feel about you. Their
comments, tastes, touches, smells may be "too rough"

for your refined systems, but that does not mean they intend to offend you.

In communicating with a thickly insulated individual, first make sure you have their clear attention. Look them directly in the eyes, sit or stand close enough so that know you are talking with them, and maybe even reach out and touch them firmly enough so that you have their full attention. Amplify your expressions and add more volume to your voice. It may feel like you are shouting or exaggerating, but this is where they are comfortable communicating.

Remind yourself they are a "more of" person and it takes lots more of what you are accustomed to using to connect with them. Once it gets through the first layer, and they become aware of the situation or your needs, they can be very responsive. It just takes more stimuli and more time for it to reach them.

If the person has less of this trait than you do; they have a thin first layer of skin and you have a thick first layer of skin:

If you know ahead of time, before you meet with this thinly insulated person, be sure to avoid wearing heavy colognes or perfumes and take extra care about your hygiene. Do not pick a noisy, bustling restaurant in which to meet. Also, wear softer understated clothing rather than bold, blazing and bulky. Best not to wear fabrics that will be scratchy or abrasive to their skin if you will be touching them.

As you meet them, make your handshake genuine but gentle. Avoid coarse jokes and raucous laughter as it will be taken as lack of respect for them. Tone down all the ways in which you interact with them. Make your verbal responses in a tone that is soft and gentle. Remember they will quickly sense if your tone is critical. Turn down the volume of your expression as well. You won't need to make bold sweeping gestures and punctuated tones.

Thinly insulated people are very sensitive to irritating noises because it takes a lot out of them to try and filter out the noises, leaving less of them to be able to stay focused upon you.

Therefore, it would be wise to select a protected environment in which to meet with them. Remember they are a "less of" person, physically and emotionally.

Since they are finely attuned to what is happening in their environment, they will notice temperature changes rapidly so pay attention to the surroundings. If the lighting is too bright, if the temperature of the room is too hot or cold, if the restaurant only serves food that is hot and spicy, it will affect them negatively.

They will appreciate you for asking how you can make them more comfortable. If they mention their discomforts and you do not respond to take care of their needs, they may perceive you as uncaring and their feelings may be hurt by this lack of perceived disregard. If you feel them creating distance from you, and you think they are disinterested in what you are saying, first check to see if they have all their comfort needs met. They will appreciate this! They relish quality, so dress, talk, and act in ways that pace their style preference.

Inner intent of both is to respond appropriately to external stimuli.

High scores do it more slowly and with greater input.

Low scores do it quickly and with less input.

9. ADMINISTRATIVE

Facial Trait

A keen sense and concern for material values.

Physical attribute: Highly arched bridge
of the nose when seen from profile of face.

HIGH SCORE

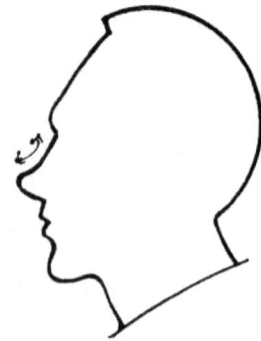

LOW SCORE

High score (8): high arched bridge of nose:

People with high arched bridge of the nose (Administrative high) are interested in and know the value of material things.

These people have an instinctive sense of the value of money. They know what their service is worth and value their time and energy. They expect to pay and be paid for services.

Their focus on monetary values makes them interested in quality, bargains, and discounts. This makes them good administrators, able to delegate and instinctively able to see where their own time would be best spent to make more money and where they can use others' services to help make or save them money. This ability to see where it is best to spend time, energy and money to make things more productive and create more monetary value is one of their strong points.

Their focus on the value of material things may make them appear to others as cold, impersonal or uncaring, especially in personal relationships. It is there that everything seems to have a price tag to their partner.

Their mate may feel they want their administrative partner to be personally generous to them, to spend time listening to them, hold them or give them personal time and energy.

The highly administrative person feels they are being generous by giving the best they can buy, by being efficient with their time and energy in order to provide their loved ones with more things, comforts and caring. This may appear to their partner as mercenary, impersonal and uncaring and cause misunderstandings in a relationship.

For the highly administrative person-

Their theme phrase is: "I know the value of my services and expect full compensation. I give and receive equal worth."

Their helper phrase is: "Let me show my loved ones my caring in a personal way, not just a monetary way."

Low Score Administrative (2) Ministrative. Concave bridge to the nose:

They automatically and personally jump in to help wherever and whenever they see a need.

People with a concave bridge to their nose are instinctively focused on human values.

This is so spontaneous that they do not stop and consider the consequences of becoming involved in whatever situation is at hand.

Their desire to be helpful is so strong that they do not assess what they actually can afford to give in terms of time, energy and money. They tend to have a sixth sense about what needs to be done for others' comforts and yet often are surprisingly unaware of their own needs and rarely assess if they should be helping at all.

Helping people on a one-to-one basis and making other people feel comfortable brings them a sense of joy and accomplishment. They are the true humanitarians in the world.

They perform their services without regard for monetary pay; many do not even care if they get paid. Therefore, they are not realistic about their time, money and energy.

Since they do not put a worth on their services, others do not either. Frequently their helpful natures are taken advantage of by other people. They sometimes offer and begin helping even when help has not been requested.

These "well meaning, overly-helpful people" need to find a way to take care of themselves first and then give of their overflow.

They must consciously become aware of not letting themselves and their loved ones be deprived of what they need for their livelihood as they often violate the principle of "pay and be paid for services."

They need to let others take care of themselves and stop helping, rescuing and doing for others what they could and should be doing for themselves.

Their theme phrase is: "What can I do to help you?" Their helper phrase is: "Let me take care of my own needs first and then give of my abundance."

Both scores want to help. High score secures others to perform needed services. Low score becomes personally involved performing services.

If the other person is higher on this trait of administrative than you (they have a high arched bridge of nose and you have a concave bridge of nose:

These people are more commercial-minded individuals; know they are more interested in how much you can save them than how you will serve them. They ultimately want the best dollar value for what they are buying or the services they are contracting. They like to pay their own way and expect you to do the same.

They can become worried and unhappy when money is not flowing in to them. Show them how you can save them money. Be sure to use numbers, in dollars and cents, to give them a clear picture of what will happen.

They do not believe in general vague terms of savings. Be specific in what they will get and what you will give and for exactly how much.

They like to get good value, especially at a discount. Show them how hiring your service or buying your product will save them.

If you are a mate, show them how purchasing a product will save your family money or why it is a bargain. They are not interested in the emotional satisfaction as the monetary savings is their emotional reward.

You may have to set guidelines of how much you will be involved and become of service since your natural tendency is not to pay much attention to the value of your time and energy. Realistically control how you spend your time, set priorities for yourself and don't get caught up into helping others with their requests for you to help with their priorities.

Be conserving of your time, energy and personal involvement since you are easily distracted by others' desires and needs. Be helpful by suggesting ideas or other resources that could help them rather than trying to do it yourself. Remember, they will respect you more when they see you value your own time and energy.

If the other person has less of this trait than you, they have a low score on administrative (ministrative) with a concave nose

and you have an arched bridge of nose, which is highly administrative:

Remember they are focused on human values. Be sure to talk about how your ideas, service or product will be helpful to them or their family.

They are not so interested in the dollar value or a bargain. They are interested in personal service, so personalize your comments. They need to feel you are a caring human being who is interested first in them as another human being.

Whatever you can do to make them feel that you care about them personally will go a long way with them. For example, bring them a small remembrance that is personal, pull a chair out for them, get them a drink of water, etc. Small gestures of personal attention feel like you care. Put yourself out personally for them. Practice expressing warmth and personal attention and caring.

Do not be too busy to take time to involve yourself in their interests also. Do not let them feel you think that they are wasting your time or that you think their values are unworthy of your support.

Find ways to make them feel special, but not with a price tag. Remember it is you who makes them know you feel they are special.

Both the high scores and low scores administrative want to be of help.

High scores do it by securing others to perform services needed.

Low scores do it by personally becoming involved in performing the services.

10. THINKING STYLE

Facial Trait

Type and timing of process when presented with new information.

Physical attribute: Slope of forehead when seen in profile. The vertical forehead is sequential thinking style; the angled back forehead is objective thinking style.

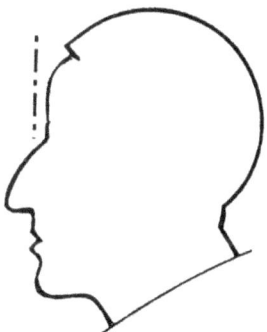

HIGH SCORE

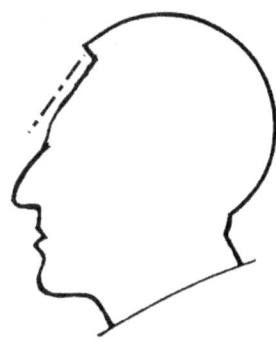

LOW SCORE

High score (8) sequential thinker: Vertical forehead; seen in profile.

People with high scores on thinking style (sequential thinkers) process new information more slowly and in a more logical, sequential manner. They like to have an orderly presentation and need more time to think things through at a much slower pace. Their thinking process is also called subjective thinking.

Because they process things in a step-by-step manner, they will stop thinking when they become stressed. Their learning style needs more time to process and understand the logic of the new information-all the way from cause to effect. It is confusing to them when they receive fragments or some of the parts are left out. They also become stressed if pressed for decisions when they have not finished comprehending the pieces of information or understood how they are connected together to make the whole picture.

If you need them to understand a new subject, situation or person, they will absorb it well if they are given time, clarity, a logical presentation and a review of the information you are presenting.

When they become stressed, they will go "blank" and not be able to think clearly or process anything more. This makes them feel frustrated and irritated and overwhelmed. If the new information is not presented in a logical sequence and they still have enough time to think things through, they will systematically reorganized what is said to them in a logical way so it can make sense to them. Although this process takes much longer, once they have understood the information, they will retain it much longer since it goes through their subjective association with the process itself and whatever they experience of its contents.

The clarity of their thinking diminishes dramatically as the amount of stressors increase. Their thinking process is located in their front brain most of the time (except when under stress). This is the conscious associational thinking that takes place whenever we are in our creative thought mode. This process takes longer. They are also inclined to think things through to safe conclusions if not under duress since their thinking style operates in the creative front part of their brain.

Historically, females have this structure to a greater degree than their male counterparts do. Traditionally, it is the female who has played the maternal role taking care of the children whose foreheads are mostly all vertical in early life.

Highly sequential thinkers benefit from realizing that not everything has to be reflected upon through a process. They can consider other's needs to act practically, quicker and more directly and encourage themselves to stop worrying if they don't get all their information organized. They should mentally rehearse themselves for new situations and learn to respond faster when others put the pressure on them.

Knowing about this style of thinking is especially valuable when working with children. Realize that they are not slow learners but that their style of getting new information is slower and configured differently. Once they have retained the new information, they can zip along as fast as anyone else can and they will remember things very well.

Their theme phrase is: "Let me think it through slowly, logically step by step first."
Their helper phrase is: "Let's cut through the long processing and act."

Low score (2) objective thinker: sloped back forehead, seen in profile.

People whose foreheads slope back are much quicker in their reactions to what is happening in the processing of new information.

Objective thinkers like to have things happen quickly. They pick up new information quickly and then apply it to what they know from the past. This allows them to come across as fast thinkers and smart since they come up with conclusions and decisions very quickly when presented with new information. They are not always correct, though, since they may miss processing much of it in their speeding along.

They may appear impatient as they tend to hurry others up because they feel pressure to slow down from others who are processing information so slowly.

They are good at the objective application of theory to immediate needs and can move much faster in the moment. Objective thinkers are processing from their back brain that holds past information, feelings, thinking.

They use their "historical archives" to bring information to the present situation to understand or solve it. They are less likely to think consciously in the moment. They are more likely to react from what they already know from their past memory, experiences or trainings.

Their theme phrase is: "Let's get to the bottom line fast."
Their helper phrase is: "Let's slow down and get the parts between the beginning and the end. I may need them."

If the other person has more of this trait than you do, (they are sequential thinkers and you are an objective thinker with vertical forehead with sloped back forehead):

They will need more time to think about what you are presenting if it is new information. Each step of the way, let them reflect on the new pieces of information. Ask them for feedback to check and make sure they understand you. They are excellent in remembering what you have told them after they have retained the information. However, it takes longer and more repetition for them to process and retain it at first.

Repeat your points in a logical and sequential manner. Do not express impatience at reviewing for them what you have already told them. They will appreciate you for the extra effort and willingness to get in step with them and feel that you care about them.

Take time to think things through and include in your verbiage the process of how you got from beginning to end. Slow down your speech rate, your gestures and your tempo.

On a personal level, you need to allow other people time to make up their own minds and at their own rate of comfort. Stay with what is happening for them instead of jumping ahead and thinking that what they are processing is not useful, applicable or practical. The process part is vital for their understanding of what you are trying to convey to them.

Give the highly sequential thinker support for the initial need to process more slowly and the ability to be freewheeling once they have fully comprehended the information you are discussing with them.

If the other person has less of this trait than you do, (the other person is an objec-

tive thinker with sloped back forehead and you are a sequential thinker with a vertical forehead):

Learn ways to look and listen more effectively when under pressure so you can move smoothly without the need to take so much time out to think and consider things along the way. Strategize ahead of time if possible to avoid becoming stressed and emotionally reactive.

Try and match some of their fast rate of delivery. Although it may feel more comfortable for you to explain things step by step, you will receive feedback that is more favorable if you will relate to the objective thinker in their style –speed up!

Talk faster, make your hand gestures more rapid and accelerate your thinking process.

If you must, list your thoughts briefly and review them until you are comfortable "winging it." You can then zip through the list quickly and this will be matching their style. Show them how you will get fast results. Quickly get to the bottom line of what you are trying to say. Otherwise, they will tire of your conversation and begin tuning you out. They do not want to be involved in the thought process from beginning to end.

Move your communication along and leave the many details of the "process" for later. As long as you have your key points covered, it will be sufficient.

The inner intent of both scores is to think things through and respond effectively.

High scores think things through logically (sequentially) and respond slowly.

Low scores (objective) think and respond quickly and reactively.

11. CREDULITY

Facial Trait

Automatically accepts things at face value.

Physical attribute: Upturned tip of nose as seen from the profile of face.

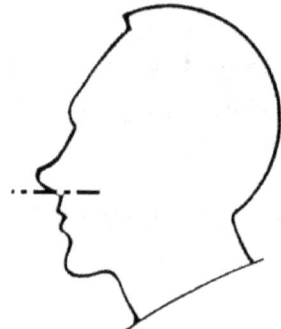

HIGH SCORE

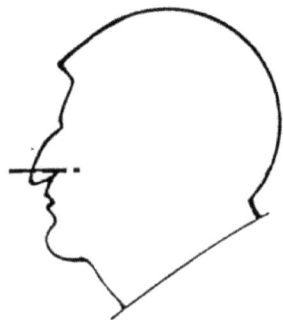

LOW SCORE

High Score (8) upturned nose, seen in profile.

They automatically accept things at face value and before proven:

People who score high on credulity automatically believe what is seen or heard. They have a childlike trusting quality, are more open-minded and receptive to what is being presented and try out new ideas without doubt or question. They are naturally inclined to be more receptive of people as they present themselves.

Because they do not check out things ahead of time, they are easily "taken in" by schemes and sob stories. It is extremely difficult for them to consider demanding answers or proof from someone they care about because they innately trust that those they love would never try and take advantage of them. After being deeply hurt, they are still inclined to be vulnerable because their trust is based on feelings instead of a thought process.

As children, we all have upturned noses and believe whatever we are told. As we grow older, a large part of the population's noses begin to turn down. However, we still see people in their later years of life with up-turned noses. Although upturned noses show an openness to believe and trust people, it creates problems where discernment is necessary.

It would benefit people with high scores on credulity to ask, "How can I prove what the other person is saying?" This would help them ask questions that would save them more than just the time it took to initially check things out before accepting them.

To other people, they may appear gullible and a pushover for anyone that comes along. Since highly credulous people are not very discerning, skeptical people may not respect them. Skeptics also disregard much of what they tell them since these high scores accept without scrutiny and do not authenticate before passing information along to others.

Their theme phrase is: "Of course, I believe it."
Their helper phrase is: "Let's check this out first."

Low score (2) nose downturned, seen in profile (Skeptical). They automatically doubt new   information.

These people automatically tend to disbelieve new things. They do not accept anything at face value and question the accuracy of everything they hear. They need lots of solid proof and check sources before they believe what you are saying. They doubt first, ask questions second; then assess what would be true from their past experiences. They automatically look for what could be wrong or what parts could be untrue. This is where their many questions begin. There must be plenty of proven facts and supporting evidence before they feel comfortable accepting something.

Every claim has to be proven – to their satisfaction. They demand proof and will take the time necessary to check out sources first. This process of checking information and people out in advance takes time, so they tend not to change or move ahead as rapidly.

They have an earnest desire to accept new ideas, information and people; however, it feels only practical and imperative for them to question thoroughly in order to discover which ideas are good and which facts are true.

To others, they may appear to be stubborn or closed minded, not receptive to new ideas, balking at good suggestions, trying to impede things from getting off the ground, stopping things in progress or even just putting a damper on the mood of creativity.

However, highly skeptical people feel they are open to new ideas, but they absolutely need to go through their questioning and scrutinizing channels to know what is true and what is false before accepting and acting on "the new."

Their theme phrase is: "I doubt that."
Their helper phrase is: "I can accept this."

If the other person has more of this trait in profile than you (they have an upturned tip of nose and you have a downturned tip of nose):

Know they will tend to easily accept what you say without questioning. They believe that there would be no reason you would not tell anything but the truth. They will easily go along with what is happening or what you propose.

Do not present a lot of facts and reference materials unless they ask for them. This will appear to them as though you feel they don't trust you. Their feelings would be hurt if someone demanded proof from them.

When they are speaking, be willing to go along and accept what they are saying. Listen openly without comments or questions. Check out the major items on which you will need to have actual proof. Let them know you do not doubt them, but you will need to have the actual documentation for your files.
Play down the importance of them proving themselves. Help them feel you are supportive and trusting of them as an individual. Because of their automatic tendencies to trust people without questioning their motives or intent, take extra care not to take advantage of them. They could be deeply hurt by any misrepresentations.

Keep your own mind more open, be more freewheeling and spontaneous when meeting with them. Leave your need for back up evidence for more significant long-range items.

When first meeting them, you will establish more rapport by accepting what they say without doubting. You can go back later on and follow through if necessary to check out their facts.

If the other person has a lower score on credulity than you do (they have a down-turned tip of nose/skeptical and you have upturned tip of nose):

Remember skeptical people tend to doubt everything new. Their doubt, however, comes from a genuine desire to accept only the things that prove valid to them.

They question every point in their minds before they consider accepting anything you say as true. It is difficult for them to take things on faith unless they measure it out, inch by inch.

Prepare yourself well ahead of meeting with them and present proof of what you are saying. Check out your facts and sources thoroughly beforehand and present supporting evidence without feeling hurt that they doubt you. Don't take their skeptical inquiries personally. They use the same yardstick for everyone else.

It is not that they do not have faith in your abilities or distrust you. Rather, it is an instinctive need to personally check out everything instead of "blindly accepting it." This instinct is on an automatic feeling level rather than a logical knowing basis.

You may see highly skeptical people as perpetual doubters, closed minded to new ideas and not open to being with people as things flow along.

Do not misinterpret them as being negative. They are actually trying to find out what the truth is. If you share freely when skeptical people are around, know that whatever you say will be under suspicion and your every word measured and scrutinized as if under a microscope.

Let them know you appreciate them taking time to make sure things check out, and that you will do your best to help them do just that. Once they have satisfactorily   accepted your information, they will be devoted, long-term, die-hard supporters of you and your product. Be patient with their process.

Inner intent of both scores is to appropriately accept new information.

High scores accept without forethought and assessment.

Low scores accept after forethought and assessment.

SUMMARY OF TRAITS
Putting the Facial Traits Together

Now, we have analyzed several key individual traits and what to do about the traits that are low to high, we can put some of them together.

Although the low and high trait scores see each other as opposites, as we are able to understand that each opposite's inner intention is exactly the same, we are able to let go of our judgment, create rapport and enjoy rewarding relationships.

When we look at a person's face, we can often see trait differences when comparing both sides of their face. Usually, this means that the parents' traits were very different. With very different trait scores on each side of the face, this person will have mood swings and a double set of gifts as well as a double set of challenges.

Our next step to understanding people by reading their faces is to learn about how their traits when studied as a whole face interact with each other.

Earlier in the book we noted how some traits will augment other traits and how some will diminish other traits. Let's take a few of the traits we have covered and see how that works.

For example, if a person is:

High on Discriminative (emotionally very selective and choosey about what and who they allow into their personal space) and is a **low score on Verbal Style** (they are quite concise, using few words and minimal sentences and descriptions) and low **score on Emotional Expressiveness** (not showing and expressing feelings easily or very much) we would find a person who appears stand offish, aloof, abrupt, may appear disinterested in what we are saying or when we are trying to get to know them upon first meeting and they would not show their feelings or even talk about feelings.

So, how warm and friendly do you think this person would appear to you at first glance? Would you rush right up to eagerly to be introduced to them? Probably not. Yet, until they let you get to know them well, you will not experience their warm, caring, loving, feeling nature that they will generously share with you as a lifelong friend.

This was an example of Discriminative trait augmented by a low score on the other two traits – Verbal Style and Emotional Expressiveness.

Let's see how **High Discriminative** works differently when the scores on **Verbal Style and Emotional Expressiveness are high** instead of low.

Although the person is highly discriminative, it is minimized by the fact that they like to talk, use many words and adjectives and they have an automatic sharing of their feelings. In other words, they usually let "pour out of them" whatever they are feeling, sad, glad, ecstatic or angry. They still like to have some reserve and choices about whom and what comes close to them; however, they appear to the outer world as being more friendly and approachable and humanized. This softens Discriminative High --the "high brow" who looks aloof and distancing.

Let's take another trait – **Innate Self Confidence-High**: In new situations, they are self-assured and will take over. They see the big picture instantly and have no fear of going into the unknown. People tend to look up to them as leaders because they present themselves so confidently. This trait is the automatic self-assured confidence that the individual is born with which will be amplified by a **low score on Toler-**

ance making them quick to act, hold self and others to high standards, scrutinizing, wants it done now, no excuses or delays; and **high score on Physical Insulation** (thickly insulated all over the body; very little gets to them; physically hardy and emotionally unbothered; well protected from the outside environment.)

This will be a person who takes charge, is undaunted by any challenge; demands everything be just right and on time. He (or she) isn't bothered by other's opinions, the temperatures or other outside influences.

Now, if you add one more trait, that of a **high score on Self Reliance**, then this same person will also want to do it "His way, or the highway." He will decide for himself what is the best course of any action, what he wants and when and will influence many others to follow him. These three other traits actually give more strength to his initial score on Self Confidence.

If, however, we give our person different supportive traits to his **high Innate Self Confidence**, the picture will change. Instead of low Tolerance, let's make him **Highly Tolerant** (he will now be more easy going, let things slide, react slower, procrastinate, forget and forgive, miss deadlines, etc.) In addition, with his new score of **low Physical Insulation,** it will make him very sensitive to the outside environment, to noises, tastes, smells and to things people will say to him and about him. It won't be easy for him to plow through new territory without feeling he has to protect himself. Also, add in a **low score on Self Reliance,** and the picture changes dramatically.

Now we have a person who is innately confident in himself; however, his easy nature will tend to put things off, be more broadminded and permissive with himself and others and not as eager to get things done and done right. His low physical insulation will also want him to protect himself from the outside influence and environment. He may not plunge forward because of the extra effort and the many unknown aspects and his low Self Reliance will make him depend on others for their opinions and support instead of first relying upon himself. These three traits will diminish his initial score on Innate Self Confidence.

Let's take one more for practice. If the person has a **low score on Administrative (they are Ministrative);** they like to personally get involved in helping others; are mostly focused on human values, want to be of personal service; not interested in monetary gain, give without regard for their time, energy and money. These are the helpers in our world. Moreover, let's add the trait of **low on the trait of Analytical,** meaning they are direct action people who don't like to mull things over and analyze all the parts before going into action. Next, let's give them a **higher score on the trait of Credulity**, which means they will believe everyone, trust automatically and not doubt what people are saying to them; even though loved ones take advantage of them, they are still willing to believe the best in them.

Therefore, now we have a person who loves to help others, even to forgetting about taking care of their own needs. Further, they don't ask for compensation for their work or seem not to value their time and all the energy they put into other people's projects and needs and desires.

Lastly, they will believe any sob story someone tells them, and jump into action to help them, regardless of what is happening in their own lives.

Although this combination of traits is seemingly the ideal person you want around so they can help you with everything, it is a great disservice to them. At some point in their lives, they need to find some balance in taking care of themselves and learning to give of their abundance, rather than depleting themselves. It is not the giving that is their problem; it is when it is out of balance that it becomes a burden rather than a gift.

Take some time to write down a trait, and see when you put another trait with it what happens. Does the first trait become stronger, or is it minimized from the effect of the second trait? You will begin to see how the composition of a personality is formed and how you can truly see that person as the unique individual that he or she is. You may start by looking in the mirror at yourself!

In our chapter At A Glance, you will find the brief summary of each of the traits we have covered for easy reference for reading people *At A Glance*.

PART TWO

"Trait Talk Stories"

or

True Stories from

Life Experiences

INTRODUCTION

True Stories from Life Experiences

All of our Trait Talk Stories are true and each story shows how our traits (when we act from our automatic inclinations) demonstrate our clear tendencies for our behavior to function from how we are structured. How we are built inclines how we are likely to automatically behave.

However, our conscious choice supersedes our structure's automatic tendencies. Once we recognize our automatic behaviors, we can make concentrated efforts to change in areas that our automatic responses are not working well for us.

As we make these conscious changes in our internal structure of operation by changing our patterns of thinking and how we act upon them, we will see that the physical features on our faces (our structure) actually change also.

These physical changes are scientifically measurable and easily recognized. We can also see the "trends" that our lives will continue to take if we do not make changes that would be beneficial to us.

Here are some of the many stories we have been privileged to collect throughout the years of working with real people in real life situations. These stories will give you some insights on how their traits worked from their   automatic responses initially and then how their choices to make changes for bettering situations that were difficulties in their day-to-day living consequentially changed their lives and relationships for the better.

Although the people named in these stories are from real life experiences, their names are changed to allow them privacy and without their written permission, we would not use their identity to tell their stories.

If you reflect carefully on how each story shows that their traits are speaking louder than their words, you may find it easier to identify which "personality trait" is speaking.

This will allow you to listen with a different mindset when you are engaged with another person in conversation, trying to understand their point of view, solving a problem, establishing rapport, creating a new alliance; anywhere you deal with people face to face.

It is important in our stories to remember that human beings are a composite of many traits and many different scorings of each trait. Therefore, the stories represented deal with only one individual trait each time. This is a simplified introduction of each trait to bring home the point of how each trait works when on automatic responses.

After we understand each individual trait (almost like an alphabet to understanding the words of our personality), we can then combine the traits. Then we see what happens when we bring two, three, ten traits together in one individual; and what happens when that composite meets another person with their totally unique (and changing) personality traits.

At this point, it is exciting to see how each one of us is a unique human being and that no other person is exactly like us with the same identical makeup and traits. (Identical twins have a special consideration.)

It is important to remember that in a close relationship, whether it is parent, partner, mate, business associate, or anywhere you daily deal personally with familiar people,
a small difference in the scoring of a trait will seem like a huge difference between two people.

It has been likened to looking at the design of a rug with your nose only two inches away from the rug versus standing back six feet away from the rug while looking at the   design. The closer you get to it, the bigger the differences will seem to appear between two people.

For now, let's take a look at some of the individual traits and how you might recognize them in another person or in yourself.

We call these "meet and greet" traits. They are traits you can easily identify as a person is walking towards you. This is seeing people - face to face - at first glance.

This section-Trait Talk Stories- of our book tells "their stories;" which may be partly your story also as you identify with some of their experiences.

1. DISCRIMINATIVE

High vs. Low

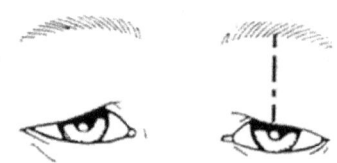

HIGH SCORE

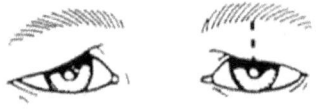

LOW SCORE

This story is about Jan, my friend of many years, who has a very high score on Discriminative. (Highly set eyebrows). Jan was very particular about her clothes, makeup, her choices of her home environment, etc. The choices may not have been the fashion of the year, but she had gone through a process before making the decisions of what she wished. It took Jan several hours to prepare herself for each day. She would carefully select her dress, and then spend considerable time picking out the best coordinates, her scarves, jewelry, purse, shoes, and coat. In her mind they should all complement each other.

One weekend, she invited me to go to a friend's home in upper-scaled Scottsdale for a social party. I agreed. I went over after work and took my clothes to change. I was ready in about a half hour. Jan was just beginning to apply her makeup. Since I knew that she was very selective about what makeup she wore to match her clothes, I just rested in the living room with a book. About forty minutes later, she came out looking like a model, everything perfectly applied and ensemble coordinated.

As we arrived at the party a little later than planned, Jan didn't see our hostess whom she knew. Suddenly a couple of guys came up and stood very close to us, one put his arm on Jan and began chatting up a storm. "Hi, how you gals doing tonight? How's 'bout a drink or a dance?"

I could see Jan stiffening and pulling away, her eyes wide and steeled. I merely said, "Gentlemen, we are looking for our hostess at this moment. Excuse us," and quickly escorted Jan to a space in a corner of the room that was quieter.

"What's wrong?" I asked with concern.

"Did you see that!!" She exclaimed. "How could they be so rude and crude and assumptive that we would want them to talk with us? They just came up in my face and without any introduction, without any courtesies or dignified language......What are we, anyway?"

I could see instantly that Jan's high set eyebrows told me she needed lots of time to get to know someone before they would be allowed to touch her. In addition, that she preferred someone she knows to come and properly introduce her to anyone else; our hostess would have been the proper person.

I glanced back at the "casual contactors." Yep, they both had eyebrows set very low on their faces. Both men had the low score on Discriminative (highly affable --low brows). Moreover, Jan, with her eyebrows high above her eyes was an impossible connection with them.

After Jan quieted down, I told her that it was a misunderstanding. That those impudent young men were not intentionally trying to make her uncomfortable nor in their minds being disrespectful.

I showed her the difference between the set of their eyebrows and her own highly set eyebrows and described what that meant, explaining they were just being "friendly" in their eyes, as their whole approach to life is casual and easy to get to know. They likely made friends easily
and then sorted out the ones they did not want after inviting them into their friendship circle. Jan's natural tendency would be to go through channels (namely our hostess, who would introduce her around to the right people) and then she would feel comfortable.

Jan listened carefully and sighed slightly. "I just don't like people getting in my space until I get to know them. I guess I can accept what you say, but I am still uneasy about someone being so casual upon first meeting."

"I understand Jan. You make fewer friends, yet your friends usually are lifetime friendships and very meaningful to you."

"Yes," she said, "and you are one of my special life-long friends!"

I then gave Jan a suggestion to help her when she encountered someone she didn't know well and wanted to "maintain her space" and yet not offend the person.

"When you see a person coming towards you, extend your hand straight out at arm's length, look at the person and smile. A friendly "Hello, my name is Jan Mandella," would be nice. As that person shakes your hand, then invite them to sit on a nearby chair. After they are seated, you can then choose a chair of your own, at whatever distance you need to feel comfortable in this new situation. This will accomplish two things: it will make the other person feel welcomed, and at the same time give you your personal space and help you feel like you are making the choices of the interaction.

Jan smiled and said she was very interested in trying out the technique.

Often times, the person with highly set eyebrows appears to be aloof, standoffish, and disinterested. However, they really are warm, feeling and wanting to be friendly. They just need to know they can be controlling how they will be friendly. It is the timing and space that help them most. If you try and choose how fast and how close you get to them, most likely you will lose out in knowing them at all.

2. ANALYTICAL

High vs. Low

HIGH SCORE

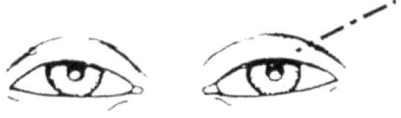

LOW SCORE

This is the story of a mom we will call Jamie and her son, Davy. I met Jamie at an elementary school where I was giving a lecture "Know Your Students by Reading Their Faces!" It was a presentation for the teachers and the parents were also invited. The subject was on how to personalize their teaching materials according to the needs of the individual students in their communications with them rather than a mass media module of teaching.

After my presentation, as customary, I stayed for anyone who would like to talk to me more privately. Mother Jamie stayed around the back marketing table displaying things for sale, then came up to me when others had left.

She approached me with this problem. She felt her son was resistive to her suggestions and her "commands." He seemed slow to do the assigned tasks and dug his heels into the ground. Sometimes he would "forget" to do his tasks completely.

With a photo of Davy, I could see exactly why. She and her son had two very dominant different traits that without understanding their primary differences could cause problematic situations for them. Here is one issue.

Mom was extremely high on the trait of direct action (this is a low score on analytical. Her eyelids were completely uncovered and showed easily when seeing her from the front. For mom, she liked a few highlights and "get to the bottom line." She liked to go into action very quickly and ...get things done! She did not like to spend much time analyzing things and "mulling them over."

As Jamie put it, "I also get so frustrated with the other teachers I work with. They can make a mountain of discussion and analyzing over nothing!!! We don't need an encyclopedia of information to make a decision about anything. Just see what it is, size up the task and get it done, I say!"

She also told me she felt the same way about her son at home, so maybe it wasn't everyone else's fault. Maybe there was something wrong with her way of thinking?

Her son's photo that she had produced from her purse with lightning speed showed a young man with traits very different from her traits. It was clear he had highly analytical thinking style (with new information) and his mom was very low analytical thinking and a majority of the time, she chose direct action after very little mental assessments.

Therefore, the mother would get bogged down if she was made to consider too many facts and figures. For her son, he would feel like he couldn't move or a make a decision unless he had enough facts to satisfy his need to "get the whole picture" before acting.

This one trait in a close relationship could cause difficulties if not understood. In addition, since she was being the m1om, it was up to her to make the adaptation until she could help her son know what it meant.

I explained to Jamie that her son, when presented with new information, processed things differently and at different speeds than she did. He couldn't feel comfortable until he had enough information to "get the whole picture" and then once the entirety of the picture came into focus for him, he could make a decision given enough time to mull it over.
He would need lots of pieces to put the picture puzzle together in his mind and then time to think about it, BEFORE he made a decision or opinion about something.

"Further," I mentioned, "the same difference seems to be at play at school for you, Jamie. Look and see if you are surrounded by many teachers who are highly analytical—and differ from your natural style of thinking."

Now, how can you deal with these similar situations?

First know you won't get anywhere by pressuring them and trying to ramrod them into faster outcomes. I suggest you can announce your own style. You could say something like, "I work best when given a new task, to just get the highlights – the key points of

it—and then go into action, either by the job completion itself in mind, or with a decision about the issue.
It is difficult for me to sit and analyze things over and
over. I become frustrated with the project itself then. I
understand some people will feel comfortable when
they are able to dissect more of the pieces and discuss and think over the pieces of the project before
beginning it. So, I am wondering if I could present the
overview of the project when we have one, and then
someone else could come in with all the details and
discussion."

"I think that could work," Jamie said with a humorous smile. "...and what about my son?"

"IF you would tell your son WHY you want such and
such done or in a particular way, Jamie, it would be
easier for him to get in step with your needs.

I replied, "Think of the project. Write down the who,
what, where, when, whys of the task at hand. Write
down the objective or the result you wish. This will
aid your son to streamline the task at hand rather
than amplifying it because of so many questions he
might come up with.

Give it a time frame, one that you can extend from
your normal active short-range. Sit down with your

son and show him what has to be done, what you wish in the end, and how much time is allowed for it. Let him sit with himself and think about it, and write any questions he has for you about the logistics of it. That way you won't be involved in the step-by-step process, which tends to bog you down, and he will be able to think about things and write them down. When he is finished "processing," you can take a highlighter and mark the key things you wanted to make sure are covered. Presto! Now let him follow through on the project after your explanation.

Praise him for seeing the big picture and the key important things that you have highlighted, so that he can stay focused on the important things, not all the other pieces that have too much detail.

Resist the temptation to "do it for him" because it may be taking longer than your normal comfort level. Recognize that it is difficult for him and that his resistance has been because he didn't see the whole picture and get to think enough about things. Help him learn that there comes a time when you must just "go ahead and take action," do your best with the information you have gathered and then, if need be with new information, you can change your course of action."

Jamie thought about this for a moment (why did that not surprise me?) and said, "Good, I will get on it right away this evening. And now that I know it is a basic style of thinking difference between me and much of my world, I can relax more as I will expect more questions from them. They also need more information and time to think things out."

'Good,' I thought. 'A good start.'

3. EMOTIONAL EXPRESSIVENESS

High vs. Low

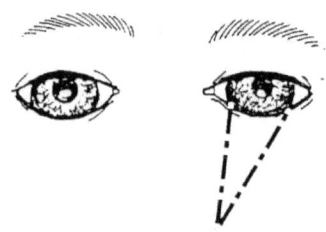

HIGH SCORE

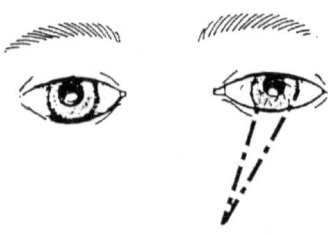

LOW SCORE

This story about Pamela and Adrianna shows how the trait of emotionality is expressed very differently in each of them.

Pamela had very large irises (her eyes when open show almost all colored in green; and very little white showing around the irises.) Pamela's feelings were always very close to the surface and readily expressed no matter what the circumstances.

Adrianna, on the other hand, had lots of white showing in her eyes and very little colored portion of the eyes. Her irises were much smaller.

How this demonstrated itself when the two girls were together went something like this:

At a mutual friend's wedding, Pamela was crying because she was so happy for her friend. "It is such a beautiful ceremony!" she said gushing and crying. Still sniffling, she added, "And the couple looks so much in love. Oh, and such a "loverly" ceremony too!"

Adrianna whispered uneasily, "Get a grip on yourself. It is just a wedding. Control your emotions, be happy for them but it's embarrassing to be gushing all the time." Adrianna at times had to go away from her because she was so uncomfortable with her friend's public display of emotions.

Her friend Adrianna felt embarrassed by Pamela's constant outbursts of emotions. "Up and down the roller coaster," Adrianna would say to Pamela. In addition, she would feel uneasy about her public display of effusive emotionalism.

Adrianna preferred to "be cool and controlled with her emotions." She felt that using her head instead of being led around by the emotions of the heart was much better. She was much more comfortable being logical than emotional and felt uneasy when people would "pry about her personal feelings." She considered it rude and at the very least a personal and private matter.

To each other, Pamela thought Adrianna didn't have much feeling, was "cold and impartial and lacked compassion." To Adrianna, her friend Pamela looked like she just puddled at any little thing and didn't have much control at all over her emotions.

I could easily see how these two friends found themselves at odds with each other because of their opposite scores on this trait of emotionality.

I showed each of them how the other one experienced the trait inside. Pamela being high on emotionality, whatever she felt, it just poured easily and fully out of her. Adrianna, being low on the score still felt things deeply and emotionally, but she did not have the automatic outpour. It was more controlled and kept more for her "personal inside life" rather than the public display.

They both had deep feelings, genuine and caring, but one made them easily overtly expressed and the other shared thoughts differently. When she was comfortable and felt safe with someone, she could share some of her feelings.

Both then felt better about themselves and each other. They felt they had come to understand their friend better. They are still friends today, and gently tease each other if they get too serious about the other's style of expressing emotionality, remembering both of them feel things deeply; one expresses them easily and quickly; the other is more guarded and at ease with logical thoughts instead of talking about emotions. Both are valid.

In addition, if Pamela wished to help Adrianna feel more comfortable in public, she could work on controlling her emotions a little more. For Adrianna, she could work on sharing more of her emotions with Pamela instead of being so reserved. Both of the ladies could help the other learn more about what was natural for each of them.

4. TOLERANCE

High vs. Low

HIGH SCORE

LOW SCORE

This story shows how when people's eyes are set very close together (inside left eye to inside right eye), they are very specific and it takes less time for them to act on what they feel or think. When a person's eyes are set far apart, they are more general, see with a broader view and longer for them to act on what they see or thinking about.

Ron's eyes were so close together you could hardly see much space beyond the bridge of his nose. He was married to Teena, whose eyes were set very far apart. She had much more space between her two eyes.

Constantly in their marriage, he would be getting upset about things not being done "right" or on time, left undone, or even simply being punctual. For Teena, if they were to be somewhere at 8pm, it surely did not mean on the dot of that time. For her, it was something to generally get close to; arriving a half hour or forty-five minutes later was not an issue, but an acceptable arrival time. She seemed to him to have no concept of the passing of time, which constantly frustrated her husband.

Ron was forever pacing the floor while she was still getting dressed and putting on her makeup. He was very specific when he told her what to do and how to do it and when to get it done but rarely did it come out that way.

Teena lived to a different drummer. That being, that there was no urgency to anything; and everything would pretty much be gotten done eventually, so why all the fuss? To her, Ron seemed like he was always impatient, on pins and needles, upset constantly about everything around him or busy trying to make others at his business be accountable for their actions.

He was an accountant with perfectionist skills., which made it very important to be precise. It would have been wise for Ron to keep his natural skills (low tolerance and a couple others) at work, and leave it there, but he would bring them home with him and begin finding faults that he felt duty bound to point out to his wife.

This caused rifts and a lot of hurt feelings because he felt he was doing the "right" thing; and she felt that he was uncaring and did not love her or he wouldn't treat her that way.

Basically, Ron thought and acted in "specifics" while his wife felt and acted in "generalities—she had a more "live and let live" attitude towards life. She was easy to be with as she could be accepting and more tolerant of mishaps, of people being late and not getting things done when they were supposed to be done because that's how she was built to function.

Ron could be counted on to keep his word to the letter of the law. He was always punctual and took seriously his commitments if he gave his word to do something. He also took it personally when other people acted so cavalier and changeable about their promises or did not follow through on their commitments.

Understanding and working on this one trait was a key turning point in their relationship.

I presented it this way to them: If we were to film a western movie, Ron sees the Indians up on the ridge in the distance and instantly and specifically sets about getting ready for the raid. He feels the imminent danger and acts as if they are already inside the fort and in "his face."

Teena, on the other hand, sees the Indians on the ridge and yawns, feeling no pressure to do anything as they are still "far away." She might say, "We'll get to them when they are much closer; no sense in getting all riled up now. Besides, they may decide not even to come down here and attack us." Therefore, she procrastinates and takes action when things are much more "up close and personal."

If these two people were enlisted officers in the army together, there would be many arguments between them as to what would be the right solution and especially how soon it should be deployed. I could see both of them nodding.

I used this metaphor to explain how each of them felt and acted, with no judgment as to which was right or wrong, they both could identify with "their soldier." I then invited them to see if they could feel what the other "soldier" must feel as their opposite. It was with some success; they both said they could get the picture. I further explained that they both had the same goal; that being they both wanted to access the situation at hand; then take appropriate action to handle it. One did it with very little time needed; the other did it with more time needed.

For their home life, I suggested they both agree on certain aspects of the home under each of their care. For example, the activity room that held her sewing machine, painting supplies and craft table, could be "her 10 acres."

This meant that Ron wasn't to comment on how clean, cleared or pristine it was. She could come out, close the door, and.....behind closed doors, she would get to the clutter in her own timing. This closed off area would not be his concern.

The den off the living room was gifted to Ron. He would move in there with his overstuffed chair, the books he loved and his flat screen HD TV along with his office files and desk. This area would be "his alone". So, each had their private areas so that they could feel comfortable whenever they wished to have things their way. Each would feel that in some area of their living, their comfort was created and respected by the other.

The common areas, the living room, the dining room, the front room, were to be kept in order to be able at any time to invite guests into their home without either of them feeling impinged upon.

The kitchen was still up for negotiation as we closed our chat, for it required more design. At least each of them had gotten something for themselves and for each other.

Teena was now aware of the stress she set up for him about never being dressed on time; so she would ask him to get her started one hour beforehand. In addition, Ron would work on being more easy-going in social situations and think about the fun they would have instead of counting the minutes ticking away.

Ron learned he had choices. For example, they agreed that if she was more than fifteen minutes late for getting out the door, he could go ahead to the function in his own car and she could follow in hers. It was such a simple idea, but both of them brightened up with the suggestion.

Sometimes it does not require that we redo our lives, but that we find one small way to change our habits to make things work out for both parties.

We met several times again, noting situations in daily life (for we are never faced with the generalities, we are always faced with the specifics in our daily lives.) They became curiously interested in situations where they would now know how the other person was feeling and could see these from the other perspective, and they became excited about how they could think of solutions more easily.

It became a game that they shared as they cared for each other and had the welfare of the other person in the relationship. Ron continued to ardently use his close tolerance skills at work where he could shine and they served him well.

Ron and Teena became more and more conscious of handling differently the areas at home that were most

important to their partner, making life more rewarding for both of them.

5. SELF-CONFIDENCE

High vs. Low

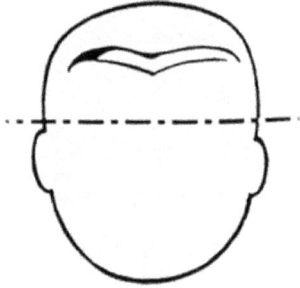

HIGH SCORE

LOW SCORE

In this story about innate self-confidence, high vs. low, we find Jerry is a high score on Self-Confidence. He is a very broad shield faced man (wide through the eye sockets as compared to the height of his face, to the natural turn of his forehead). Instinctively, Jerry will handle almost anything that comes along without having to do anything ahead of time to prepare for it. The opposite of Jerry was Paul.

Paul came to work for Jerry. Paul had a long and very narrow face (very low on Self-Confidence.) Paul's face looked much like the sign of a cross when measured through the eye sockets to the length of his face, and Jerry's face was much like a plus sign.

Both men were in the business selling household goods to small chains of stores. Paul had recently been hired by the company's personnel department and placed under Supervisor Jerry.

After only a few days, Jerry called me and was complaining to me with dismay about his new recruit's work. I asked him what specifically was not fitting for him. He mentioned a number of things, mostly pointing to this issue: he saw Paul as timid, hesitant, and unable to grasp the big picture and run with it; holding back a lot, and reticent about taking on projects and new tasks himself. In addition, that he didn't see Paul eager to make cold calls. Jerry pointed out Paul seemed to always wait for him to tell him what to do and how to do it.

I looked at Paul's personnel photo and could instantly guess why they were having these difficulties.

Paul and Jerry were just about as opposite as you could find on the scoring of innate self-confidence.

Jerry, with his high score on confidence, thought in very big pictures, talked with broad and sweeping gestures, visualized overwhelmingly large goals and directives, expecting that Paul should be on the same page as he and "run with it." Jerry further was undaunted by anything, coming into new situations cold and just "finding a way to get it done by rising to the occasions."

I showed Jerry that Paul was built to function naturally with smaller projects, was hesitant to accept responsibility without preparing well for it, needed more narrow focused instructions and that he worked well in a supportive environment instead of out doing the main leadership.

I invited Jerry to "chunk it down" for him; give him only the first part of the project, give him support and praise for each completion and let him feel that he was making a significant contribution.

I stated that Paul would be a good student and a very loyal employee. He could follow directions very well and was very conscientious but he couldn't do well when he felt that Jerry was coming at him like a steamroller and overpowering him, making him feel intimidated.

Jerry agreed to follow the suggestions I then gave him.

It was about one month later when Jerry and I spoke and he expressed his appreciation for helping him understand the differences between them because now he could utilize Paul's natural skills where they would do the best work for his company.

Jerry further saw the benefit for his entire company and we did profiling for each of the employees and made recommendations to further enhance the natural gifts and talents of each of the employees.

We then did training for his staff so that they also could be aware of themselves, their peers, and better know and understand their customers and their needs.

In the training, Paul was able to understand why he initially felt the way he did, and to make some changes in his way of approaching people who were built much like Jerry.

From this training, Paul gained more confidence. In the training he also discovered that his confidence is called "earned confidence levels" and although he wasn't innately born that way, with practice, he also could rise to challenges and prepare ahead of time to take on projects that were larger than he was accustomed to handling.

The other employees were very appreciative of the new ways of reading people...before they spoke... by reading their faces.

One employee said, "Everyone expects us to look at their face so it makes it so easy to get in step with them and know them from the inside out. My sales have increased significantly because I can read what is best for them, rather than what I think is best to sell them."

6. SELF-RELIANCE

High vs. Low

HIGH SCORE

LOW SCORE

In this story, a mother named Marianne was complaining about her young ten-year-old son who she could not get to do the simple task of taking out the garbage. Marianne had a low score on Self Reliance (her nostrils were very close set) and her son Ryan was very opposite with a high score on Self Reliance (his nostrils were extremely flared out from his nose.)

She confessed that she was almost too embarrassed to discuss her seemingly inadequate ability to control her son. She reported that she never had any problems following directions and complying with household chores or school assignments when she was a kid. She was "a good kid and very obedient."

She further stated that Ryan was generally a good kid, was able to entertain himself, was her youngest child, and played fine with his siblings; yet, he seemed to balk when it came time for him to do his assigned chore of taking out the garbage. She also admitted that his teacher had called her. She was not only mystified but also frustrated as well about Ryan's balking at being told what to do.

I asked to look at a photo of him, and Marianne produced a family photo taken a few months ago. There was her son Ryan, with a very high score on self-reliance. Here was a young man, not only going through the early changes physically, but his dominant trait was self-reliance and everything inside of him propelled him to "do it his way." He wouldn't like someone telling him what to do and wanted to rely upon himself instead of others. He had a fierce sense of autonomy and felt immense pressure when someone told him his was "doing it wrong or they knew a better way than what he thought."

This part of his personality was getting in the way of his schoolwork sometimes, because he would hand in assignments that were done not to the exact specifications of the teachers, but in his own style of expression and thoughts.

I pointed out to Marianne that she had a low score on self-reliance so it made it easier for her to follow directions. She could rely on others to make decisions and generally be a good student and follow the guidelines of those in charge.

Mom Marianne had already been called into the school for a parent-teacher conference, since he was marked down in grades for not doing his assignments the way the teacher had instructed them to be done.

I suggested that before we involve the teachers, we talk about it together. She was very relieved. I could tell that she did not like negative attention.

At our meeting, I explained to her that Ryan's key dominant trait was his high score on self-reliance. Further, I described how it felt inside of him when he felt his own "independent thinking or choices" were restricted or taken away from him – it felt like he had lost his freedom and respect. He really feels inside that he wants to make his own decisions and direct his own life; not "under the thumb of someone else." As for a solution, I said, "Marianne, what would happen if you took the simple chore of emptying the garbage and change your way of requesting that of him?"

"How?" she asked.

"Well, if you explained to him that emptying the garbage was essential to keeping the operation of the household running smoothly, but that you don't have an idea of how it would best be done. Could he figure out some way of getting a routine set up? Just see what he comes up with." I knew Ryan had lots of creative thinking and was also analytical.

Marianne took my advice, went home and talked with Ryan. The next week she was chuckling as she called me with this report: Yes, he did take the suggestion (instead of the command sounding like an authoritative demand) as a golden opportunity to do things "his way."

He "ordered" a large poster board and marking pens. Upon which he produced "a schedule" of when he would be picking up the wastebaskets in the kitchen, bathrooms and common areas. The bedrooms of each family member were the responsibility of each person who slept there to empty their own wastebaskets into the large one downstairs. If they did not, they wouldn't be carried out to the trash barrel and taken out to the curb. He carefully made a chart and posted it so everyone could see what he was doing and when the emptying of the trash from the house would take place. Further, they were to do their share by making sure their own wastebaskets were ready to go out.

His mom said she could see that Ryan now took some pride in his project instead of feeling as if it was punishment and an assignment from someone in authority.

"All I wanted to do is get the task done, but you have made it so he is feeling good about doing it and even a bit bossy at times. But that is okay by me," she said with a tone of amusement in her voice.

We then went to school for a meeting with his teacher and applied the same operation. We discovered there were assignments that could have leeway and creative approaches, and then talked with Ryan so he could be aware that he was choosing to do the best he could. Sometimes that meant choosing to do it their way, and those other assignments he could get the same result, but by doing it his way. It was really a metaphor for life, his mom explained.

Ryan seemed to accept the school assignments better. Maybe it was because at home he could "rule his own ten acres of the operation of disposing of their garbage—his way."

7. VERBAL STYLE

High vs. Low

HIGH SCORE

LOW SCORE

This story involves two salesmen, Don and Peter, who worked at the same company.

Don had a very high score on verbal style; his upper lip was extremely full. Peter, on the other hand, had a very thin upper lip; he had a very low score on verbal style.

Don's normal inclination was to open his mouth, start talking and form his thoughts as he took his listener on a very long journey through his thoughts, rather like a shaggy dog story with lots of detail, colorful descriptions and many long sentences.

Peter, on the other hand, was extremely concise with his communications. With his extremely thin upper lip, he thought about what he wanted to say, and then very briefly and quickly expressed it.

These two men were instructed by their boss to collaborate on some articles to be published in their corporate newsletters.

They had agreed to each write one article; then they would have the other one edit the article before presenting it to their CEO.

When Peter and Don completed their articles, they set about the editing. Peter was stunned to find that Don's article was ten pages long! Don was dismayed to see that Peter's article was only four paragraphs long.

Each man felt he had sufficiently covered the subject required in the appropriate amount of words. Don, with his thick upper lip was inclined to write a long letter.

Peter with his very thin upper lip felt he did best streamlining words and "cutting to the chase" and wrote like a western union telegram – briefly; just the facts.
Therefore, when Peter edited Don's article he cut, cut, and cut! When Don edited Peter's article, he expanded, added and expanded some more.

When both men saw their edited versions, they were not very pleased. They felt the other's editing destroyed what they wanted to impart to the company's readers.

Since Don was a friend of mine, he called me and expressed his great disappointment. He told me that they only had two more days before they had to turn in their articles, and he could not let his article be "slaughtered down to nothing."

I asked him if Peter had a very thin upper lip. He said, "Yes!" I could hear questions in the tone of his voice.

I knew that my friend had a very thick upper lip, so I began explaining the difference between their verbal styles, which would also transfer into the way they wrote words. Don being concise, Peter using more words.

Don agreed but did not see how that would resolve the conflict that had arisen. I then suggested what I always call, "the third alternative." It is another solution other than the two ways being presented.

I suggested that they propose to their director that the company publish a book, expanding the subject matter in depth (Don's natural tendency style) and that Don continue to write his long versions (keeping the long version for the book) and that Peter continue to edit these, thus presenting their boss with a short acceptable version for short articles.

In addition, if the company wanted to, they could have a website link from the articles to the longer versions which would be forthcoming as a compete book.

Don was excited about the idea and said he would talk with Peter and his CEO.

One day later, I received a call from Don thanking me for the suggestion. He said Peter was much relieved and Don reported that his boss was not only appreciative of the idea, but also excited about implementing the suggestion into their company policies.

He further said that at the next company meeting, he would present both of them with a certificate of appreciation for their proposal of both the articles and the book, which the company would publish and give them credit for authorship.

I felt good that both writers would be recognized for their talents and that they both felt positive about honoring the use of their natural skills.

It was another reminder that we can often find solutions to our differences when we understand the nature of each person's trait opposites and look towards a collaborative way to get both parties' needs met. Things are often not black and white, not one side or the other side.

Finding solutions to a situation that includes the best of both sides is what I like to call "the third alternative."

8. PHYSICAL INSULATION

High vs. Low

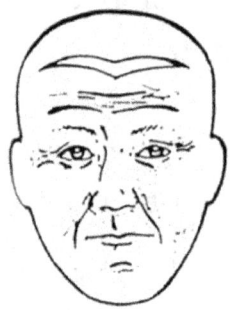

HIGH SCORE

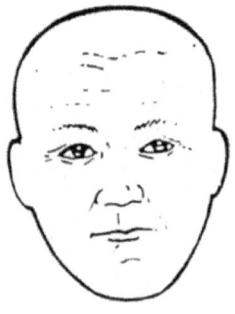

LOW SCORE

This story shows how two men had very different scores of physical insulation (one high score - a thick first layer of skin and the other man had a low score - very thin first layer of skin) and how their vastly different scores of physical insulation affect them in their lives. Both men were musicians and both men hired the same agent, Dawn, to promote their bookings.

As a well-known promoter of musicians, Dawn prided herself on getting "great gigs" for her clients that also paid well. She had represented the two clients that we mention in this story for a couple of months.

One musician played the fiddle and the other one played the guitar. Both men had been playing in the local pubs. Dave was having a wonderful time and could not have been more pleased with his bookings. Sal, on the other hand, was struggling to get through his performances and was exhausted at the end of each night.

Dawn asked me my opinion of what she could do to help Sal be more enthused and positive about where she had placed him. She felt his disenchantment and took it personally.

As soon as I saw the promotional brochures of the two men, I knew instantly what the biggest problem was.

Dave was thickly insulated. His rugged exterior physically "shielded him" from the outside environment.

The smells of the bars didn't offend him. He didn't even notice the loudness of the crowd in front of him as he was playing. He relished thinking up come-backs for those hecklers from the back of the room. Some of the patrons smoked, but it did not bother our rugged guitar player, Dave. He never personalized things customers would say, and actually found "just the right song to banter back at them." When the crowds hooted and hollered, he took that as his sign he was doing very well at getting them involved in his presentation. Dave was actually energized at the end of the night when he went home.

Sal was the opposite. His eyes and nose stung from the smoke. He was distracted by the door opening and closing every time someone entered or left the club. He personally felt affronted that people would be talking and laughing at times during his performance. Hecklers in the room almost paralyzed him with fear and frustration and he personalized their interrup-tions. He found it hard to jump from his chosen list of prepared songs to the spontaneous requests hollered out to him from the audience during his performance.

At the end of the night's performance, Sal was so ex-hausted that he barely made it home. He could not even function until just before going on stage again the next night. He was ready to quit, but he really needed the job.

Dawn asked me to come in and consult with her on finding a solution. When I saw their promo photos, I exclaimed, "Of course! Of course Sal has such problems with the bookings you have placed him in."

She looked stunned and curious at me, "Of course....what?!" She asked.

I explained to her that both were great musicians, but they needed totally different environments in which to play their music. Dave was thickly insulated and was perfectly suited for the place he was playing. His natural "insulation" protected him physically, mentally and emotionally.

Sal, however, needed to be playing his music in a very protective environment. He needed not to have lots of outside environmental interferences, such as noises, people side talking, smoke, and interruptions. I told her it would be best to book him into church events, private quiet afternoon ladies' functions, educational presentations, or private parties that were quiet and desirous of just listening to his music alone; somewhere there would be no side talking.

"His skin (physical insulation layer) is very thin. He has very low level of insulation to protect him," I explained to Dawn. "Everything from the outside gets to him quicker and impacts him more. He needs a "less of" environment to feel comfortable so he can concentrate on what he is doing. He can then put all his energy into playing his music, rather than trying to shut out all the things that are bothering him so much.

Then Dawn showed me a promo video of Sal's presentation. I pointed out to Dawn how sensitive he was by showing her how his eyelids even fluttered when he played various parts of the songs. His fingers also tenderly touchede the instrument he was playing. I suggested that she find some places that would be quiet and refined in the environment for him to play his music.

I received a phone call from Dawn several weeks later. She told me how Sal now loved his bookings at the churches and the quiet museum functions. She had even booked him into the Irish Museum's fundraiser and discovered that he loved playing his Irish music. Sal told Dawn that he felt the new audiences "appreciated him." He even asked her to book more for him. He was now filled with lots of energy at the end of the night from performing, instead of being so depleted.

Dawn was so pleased at this dramatic change in Sal. However, the change was actually in placing him in the right environment to perform his music.

The solution I suggested to Dawn came from my noticing only just one physical trait of her performer Sal...his physical insulation. This trait is such an important one to understand because it covers our entire body- from tip of toes to top of head.

9. ADMINISTRATIVE

High vs. Low (Ministrative)

HIGH SCORE

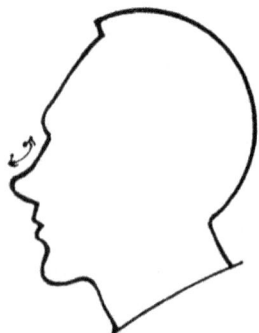

LOW SCORE

This is the story of Ryan and Pam. They had been together for about one year. The intense honeymoon
dazzle had worn off and now in the routines of mar-

ried life, they faced the day-to-day questions of how do "we live well together."

By the time Pam came to me for counseling, they both were ready for divorce. She knew she loved Ryan, but found it exasperating living with him because day-to-day issues continued to appear.

She produced their wedding photo for me to see. I could readily see that they had three major trait differences that were never recognized by them before they got married. Here we will cover one of the traits. Pam had a very low score on Administrative (she loved being personally involved in helping other people on a one-to-one basis. Her primary focus was human values and she got personally involved in helping people.

Her husband was the opposite. He was highly administrative, efficient with managing money and people and
focused on the efficient ways to get things done. Often it was at arm's length from personally doing things.'

She said to me, "I feel he is so uncaring and focused on making money or scrimping on spending money. He never gets me anything if he can't write it off as a tax deduction for his business. I feel as if I am a client rather than his wife."

There were tears in her eyes as she told me this. I could see that this issue caused her a great deal of strain for some time.

Pam continued, "When I was sick in bed, what did he do? He sent some agency with a nurse practitioner to check on me, write some prescriptions, and handle anything I needed. When I asked him to make me some soup, what did he do? He had the local deli deliver some. He has this hands-off attitude for caring for me. When it is my birthday, his secretary sends me flowers – I am sure as an expense written off on his business operations."

"It is all so impersonal! I would never have called anyone else to take care of someone I love. I would have gone there myself and sat with him and given him all my care and compassion ----and the chicken noodle soup too!"

The emphatic unction in her tone was clear evidence of her level of frustration and disappointment with her husband.

Then Pam's head slumped, she covered her face with her hands and started sobbing. After a few minutes as the crying turned into a muffled sniffling, I asked her quietly, "Pam, you have shared a lot of what you don't like. Can you tell me what it is that you would like?"

It was suddenly quiet. Her head came up and her eyes met mine. Almost as for the first time she had a possible option she had never considered.

"I....ah...I ...well...." She stammered. "I guess I really want to know that he loves ME and really puts me as the important part of his life. I hear him say he loves me when I ask him, but I somehow don't feel it because of some of these things I have told you."

I suggested to Pam, that she make a list of the things that if he did them she would be sure that he loved her...no question at all. She agreed and I noted a flicker of hope in her big brown eyes.

As I set a time for our next appointment, I smiled and said, "I would like to talk to you both about some of the differences between you. Would you feel good if Ryan came with you to the next session since it involves both of you and how you want to live well together? It may be helpful to share your thoughts with him with my support. If you like...."

"Oh, yes! Yes!" Pam said, and I could see her take a deeper breath as she walked out of the room.

One week later, Pam arrived with her husband Ryan. He obviously was appearing somewhat guarded and businesslike. Ryan was dressed in his business slacks, shirt and tie. He had taken his sports jacket off as he entered the room. Ryan was definitely a high score on Administrative. Pam was equally different with her high score on Ministrative. They also had two other key trait differences, which we can cover in other trait talk stories

I decided to address their first key difference of Administrative/Ministrative between them.

I did this by asking if they would be willing to sit in chairs facing each other and with knees almost touching. When they were situated, I asked another question. Would they allow me to speak for them as if I were each of them? They both looked surprised but nodded yes.

I first stood behind Pam and looked at Ryan. Then I said, "Ryan, I have been feeling a little unsure of your love recently and I am wondering if you would be willing just to listen to me, without feeling I am saying there is anything wrong with you about what I am feeling and what I need?"

He nodded, slowly and cautiously.

"I would like to know I matter most in your life. The way I tend to know that is when the person who loves me brings flowers, he hands them to me; or if I am sick, he asks what HE can do for me that would heal me instead of sending someone else. On the other hand, if I want to talk about something, he doesn't hurry me through things. I have to know that I matter as a real person, not just a commodity."

Ryan shifted uneasily in his chair but said nothing. So I went over and stood behind him, and then looked at Pam. "Pam, here is how I see what I do to show you I love you. I work a lot so that we can have not only conveniences in our home, but also take trips, and do other fun things and save for the future."

I continued, "When I have my secretary send you flowers, it is because I wanted YOU to have them. She knows the florist I like to use and then I can keep working to pay for the flowers. It is true that I plan our vacations and extra activities so that I can do a little business, but that is so I can get business done and save more money so that I can take care of you. If I physically came over when you were sick, then I couldn't be at work and the business would falter. I might catch something from you and then I would be sick, setting us back even further. There is no one at our small business that can pick up the slack for me when I am not there, so I try to do everything myself. I use our business as a tool to help us live better and I do it because I love us. There is no one in this world that I want to be with, but you...for the rest of my life!"

I paused.

Ryan nodded rapidly and burst out saying, "That's absolutely true, Pam. She's absolutely correct! That is exactly what I am thinking."

Pam's voice was shaky as she murmured, "Oh, my...Ryan...that is all I need to know! To know you are doing it because you love me, not because you don't care about me." She was in Ryan's arms at that point, kissing his face, holding him tightly.

He laughed. "My dear sweetheart, to think that you were worried I didn't care about you! You are my everything!"

When they had settled again, I brought up the question of the homework I had assigned Pam.

She looked at Ryan first and spoke softly, "Honey, I am so relieved to know that you do these seemingly impersonal things for me because you love me! Now I see that in your thinking by staying working, you made more money by engaging others to help take care of our needs rather than you personally doing it. It makes sense to me now, from your viewpoint."

She ran her fingers down her list page after page...then set it down on her lap. "I would just like to know if you would be willing once in a great while to go to dinner together, a romantic intimate candlelight dinner without having other business people with us."
"Yes, honey, I could easily and happily do that for you. Now that you have explained to me how you feel about these things. On your birthday and Christmas, I will just get you something personal...very personal!" With that, he winked and Pam blushed.

I stood up again, a signal our session had come to a close and asked each of them if they got something valuable from the session. Ryan even said he would make a little list for Pam so that she could know what would for sure bring a smile to his face, should she wish to do something for him. He put his arms around Pam and they exited as she chatted happily.

As we look at this one trait alone, we can see how Pam, highly ministrative, would always think of the personal, one to one, involvement with people; more interested in the human values. While her husband Ryan was more interested in the administrative parts that could attain the goal of taking care of them as a couple. He found his time was more valuably spent doing his work and sending people who were qualified to care for his sick wife

Both opposites can learn from each other, and if they are in a close relationship, this difference (which when seen from opposite perspectives) can comple-ment, rather than compete with each other.

10. THINKING

Sequential vs. Objective

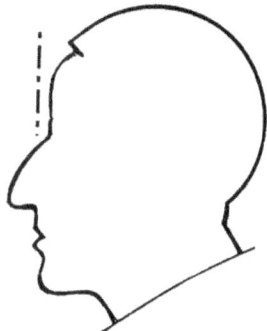

HIGH SCORE-Sequential

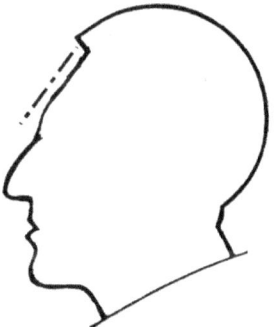

LOW SCORE- Objective

We will see in this story how a father and a son with opposite scores on this trait of thinking style caused considerable problems in the son's ability to develop reading skills.

Matthew was in the first grade. His thinking style was subjective thinking. (Seen from the profile of the head, the son's forehead was totally vertical.) Matthew was a very high score on the trait we call sequential thinking. His natural style of approaching reading was to systematically take his time one word at a time, from the beginning to the end of the story.

If he was distracted or interrupted, he would have to start reading all over again from the beginning. Matthew also did well in remembering the story if he could read the story several times so he felt he "got it." It took him longer to read the story and required more repetition, but when he read that way, he would retain it very well and completely.

The school would typically send home some reading assignments with instructions that the parent was to sit with their child and have their child read stories to practice the child's reading skills. Matthew's father, Ron, had decided that sitting with his son and letting him read to him was a perfect time to create a "bonding experience" with Matthew. Therefore, during school days, when he came home from work, Matthew would try to read to Ron.

Father Ron, however, was the complete opposite of his son's style of thinking. Ron was what we call "a fast back." His objective style of thinking was very fast. He would approach new things by quickly accessing things from his back brain (the past) and make some fast judgments and comebacks. This made him appear as though he was a very fast and smart thinker. Often though, he was so speedy that he missed some of the things in between the thoughts he sandwiched together.

It was painfully frustrating for Ron to listen to Matthew's slow deliberate and painstakingly plodding manner of reading.

Ron would say, "Hurry up, Matthew. Come on, let's move along." Then Matthew would become discombobulated and flustered and stop. Then Matthew would have to go back to the beginning and start reading again.

Ron was quickly becoming completely exasperated. His wife, Karen, called me and begged me to come over, as Ron had suggested that they take their son to a school psychologist since he obviously had something wrong with his mind. He wasn't even able to read a simple story.

Fortunately, I was able to visit their home before that type of drastic action was taken and was able to see Matthew reading to his dad. Instantly I could see the blaring problem. In addition, the solution was equally instant.

I explained their huge differences in thinking styles and told them that Matthew was not a slow learner, and it had nothing to do with intelligence. Further, that it was only a learning style, and that if they would be willing to make a small change in Matthew's reading sessions, I thought the difficulty would be dissolved. Of course, by then Ron was intrigued, and eager to have anything that would relieve him of such a painful self-imposed duty.

I suggested merely that wife Karen sit with Matthew and let him read to her. The reason was that Karen, his mom, had a similar thinking style. Her style matched her son's very well. They were both sequential thinkers. They both had foreheads that (viewed in profile) were vertical instead of fast-backed (viewed in profile sloped backwards.) Her sequential thinking style also afforded Matthew his much needed patience and time.

That solved their problem immediately, and I think that Ron was secretly thankful for the change as well as Matthew.

For the highly sequential thinker (the vertical forehead) they need the gift of time and repetition. They learn best when they see things in an outline form. Once they have it committed to their memory, it lasts. Since sequential thinkers are mostly in their front brain, which is conscious associational thinking, the creative portion of thinking, the process will naturally slow down to be able to fully assimilate the new information.

The objective thinker, coming from their back brain, quickly retrieves stored material to make sense of the new unknown things that are presented. Since it is back-brain thinking, it does not require going through the conscious associational thinking. Therefore, it appears as a fast thinkers, but not necessarily fully accurate thinking as they speed along to the response.

Both styles of thinking are assessing outside stimuli and putting it together to retain it. One does it with more processing time and in a logically sequential manner. The other requires very little processing time and may pull information from the past to under-stand or deal with the present situation.

Matthew's grades also came up as he was able to pro-cess in the way he needed. At least for this family's situation, my glance at Matthew and Ron's foreheads identified the trait that was causing the problem. With the change of giving Matthew, a sequential style listener, his mom (also a sequential thinker) we were able to solve this family's dilemma. In addition, this minor adjustment in how they went about helping their son with his reading made a huge difference in his learning abilities as he continued to grow up.

11. CREDULITY

High vs. Low (Skeptical)

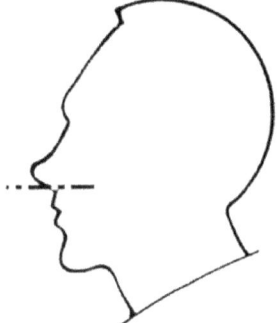

HIGH SCORE

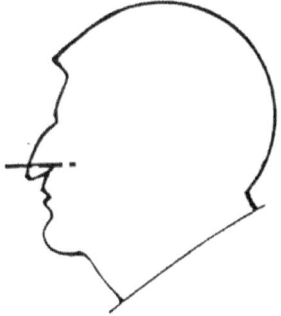

LOW SCORE

This is another true life story showing how one married person who had a high score on credulity (believes automatically what is seen or heard) appears to her partner who has a low score on credulity (is automatically skeptical to what is seen or heard.)

Angie (high score on credulity) was married to Jeff (very low score on credulity; highly skeptical.) Angie was constantly and automatically believing things she read, things she heard and especially accepting as true, whatever people said. She was especially susceptible to those around her whom she liked.

Angie believed it best to accept people at face value and be trusting and look for the best in them. She prided herself on being open minded and trusting.

Her husband, Jack, on the other hand, was very skeptical and was always doubting and questioning everything anyone said. It seemed to Angie that he disbelieved everything and automatically mistrusted everyone. It was hard for him to confide in anyone with his level of disbelief. This caused not only friction between them, but he reported that her "gullibility" was costly in other ways to their marriage.

One story he brought up in their counseling session with me was this:

Angie received a notice in the mail about a free diamond pendant being offered. She found out that she could receive this gift just calling a phone number since her name was drawn and she had won this prize. It further stated that she had a chance for a free cruise.

Angie was very excited. She had never had a diamond before and promptly called the number. An appointment was set. She went. She listened patiently for a presentation about the cruise she was entered to win. When the one-hour presentation of the "wonderful cruise to the Caribbean" was finished, she was sent over to a representative to get her diamond necklace. She then paid for shipping and handling of the diamond necklace of $12.95.

About one week later, she "received the wonderful news that her name was drawn for a free cruise to the Caribbean. She was ecstatic! She could hardly believe her good fortune. The only thing she had to do was to pay for the processing fee. She then gladly paid the presenters $49.95 for the handling fee for the package for the cruise. They handed her the information packet and she departed with high spirits and excited to share with her husband the wonderful trip they could now go on.

When she arrived home and announced her great fortune, her skeptical husband Jack frowned deeply.

She explained ardently about her coming diamond necklace, and gave him the packet about the cruise. His eyes narrowed as he began to read the "contract" she had signed. When the skeptical partner had finished, he determined it was useless, and that she had spent their money frivolously and futilely. "Worthless! Absolutely worthless," he exclaimed.

The contract required that they buy the plane tickets, buy a hotel to stay in the night before boarding the ship, pay for the surcharges of the booking and the cruise trip. And of course it did not include any of the transportation fees and the tips, and ...and....and.... In addition, the worst part of it; it had so many blackout times that it could not be used except in a few days during the year.

Further, it required that they submit their desired dates for the cruise in writing to an office in Florida listing three times they would like to travel and the request must be made six months in advance. No time was guaranteed until the company wrote back. If the three times requested were not available, the company would assign a time for them to travel.

The highly skeptical husband became outraged. The highly credulous wife became devastated and angry.

This was obviously not the first time something like this had happened between them.

From Angie's point of view, she was trying to do something wonderful for them to share...a dream come true. Now that dream had become a nightmare because of her husband's reaction.

Jack, on the other hand, had seen it as just another unthinking and ridiculously gullible thing his wife had done. He felt that she didn't care about what happened to their finances when she did careless and unthinking commitments like that. Therefore, he didn't feel that she respected their marriage.

When I counseled them, I was able to show each of them how their differences operated when they acted automatically and how they appeared to each other. I pointed out the best parts of their opposite traits of highly credulous and highly skeptical. I also showed them how each of their traits were good in some respects and worked well to take care of them: namely, that his skeptical nature could ward off being duped easily, and that her trusting nature was a real godsend in meeting with friends and family and being receptive to people's conversations.

We then made a plan for things that would affect them both in the marriage and living together.

She would come home with the "ideas" but would not commit to doing anything until she had asked her husband to check things out first. This would allow her to keep her sense of excitement and possibilities and trust alive.

He would not immediately question and doubt her, but only after reading or investigating the "real deal", he would sit down and gently go over what was really being offered and what they collaboratively would decide was in their best interests.

One week later, I received a phone call. Both of them were on the line. She said, "I found an ad for a wonderful offer for a vacuum cleaner...that did everything you needed to clean your entire house."

Then Angie laughed and continued, "I remembered what you told me to do, Annemarie." "So, I brought the ad to my beloved husband and asked him to check out the fine print."

"Yes," said Jeff. "And of course I went through it with my fine toothed mental comb. I felt good because she was inviting my best trait to go to work....my automatic skeptical nature. Therefore, I was very pleased with her for making this change instead of just automatically signing us up for things.

In reading the ad, I found out that, the vacuum itself was a pretty good deal, but that you had to sign up for the bags, and the scents, and the twice yearly servicing. When I pointed these facts out to Angie, she said, "Then that won't work for us."

Jeff said, "I felt respected by her because she was willing to let me scrutinize it ahead of time. And I even suggested that we offer to buy the vacuum cleaner if they did not make us take the rest of the deal."

"We both felt very good that we were able to use what we learned in our session with you and respectfully handled another experience together so that we both felt appreciated. That was worth the diamond necklace!" Jeff laughed.

"Yes! Me too" Angie chimed in. Then she added, "I did get the diamond necklace after all, six weeks later. It was so tiny that Jeff made it humorous by getting out our large magnifying glass and peering at the tiny chip through the glass and exclaimed..."Wow, it is a diamond!" We both laughed and hugged each other.

SUMMARY

Trait Talk Stories

We have seen through these stories how our personality traits act automatically and how they can function to our advantage or how we can be subject to their disadvantage. There is no good or bad trait. Rather, it is our task to notice when each of our automatic traits are serving us best and to redirect them when they are working against our best interests.

As we can become aware of how we are acting automatically and make some conscious choices to redirect our traits, we will find that indeed our physical characteristics (the features on our faces) actually change and can be scientifically measured and verify changes we have made for ourselves.

The changes we make on the inside will be shown in our physical structure on the outside of our bodies. Some traits change very quickly and some like bone structure take longer to show up.

Now, let's take a quick glance at our traits in brief review – in the next section called "At A Glance."

PART THREE

At-a-Glance Traits, a quick look at Facial Traits

Introduction

to At-A-Glance

This section of the book covers information on each trait in a concise brief overview. It is a handy reference that will give you the key things to remember about the trait—at a glance.

At the bottom of the page, find some space for you to look at yourself and NOTE where you are in the scoring from 1-10. Remember, no score is better than the other is; it is just different and augments or diminishes other traits when you put all your traits together-- later.

So, let's take a look at some of what I term the Meet and Greet Traits; some of the features that you can easily see as someone is walking towards you or easily identify as your own traits when looking in the mirror.

We begin with the upper part of the forehead, work our way down the front view of the face, and then go to your profile (seen from the side of your face.)

We will cover these traits: Discriminative, Analytical, Emotionality, Tolerance, Self-Confidence, Self-Reliance, Verbal Style, Physical Insulation, Administrative, Thinking, and Credulity.

1. DISCRIMINATIVE

At-a-Glance

Timing of instinctive, emotional selectivity.
Physical Attribute: distance of eyebrows above eye.

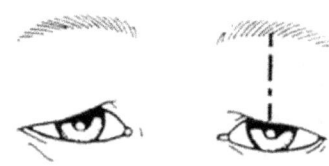

HIGH SCORE

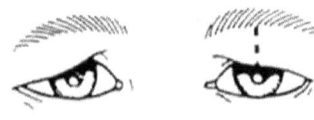

LOW SCORE

High Score

- ✓ Very selective of choices before being involved
- ✓ Takes more time to know others
- ✓ Needs more space
- ✓ Appears aloof, reserved
- ✓ You must earn their closeness
- ✓ Likes to control style of interaction

- ✓ Maintains lifelong fewer friendships from ones accepted
- ✓ More formality

Low Score

- ✓ Fewer distinctions and easily involved
- ✓ Easy to know when first meeting
- ✓ Close up okay
- ✓ Appears approachable
- ✓ Makes friends easily, quickly
- ✓ More easily flexible in new meeting
- ✓ Becomes intimate soon; makes choices after being involved
- ✓ Acts/dresses casual

BOTH want to: make valid emotional selections.
High score does before becoming involved.
Low score does it after becoming involved.

2. ANALYTICAL

At-a-Glance

The need to process (analyze) things before acting.
Physical Attribute: Fold of skin covering eyelid.

HIGH SCORE

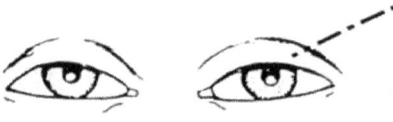

LOW SCORE

High Score

- ✓ Analyzes, compares; questions, investigates
- ✓ Needs to process first
- ✓ Needs lots of info to get full picture
- ✓ Slow processing, resists deciding without all the pieces, appears stubborn

Low Score

- ✓ Doesn't like analyzing, comparing
- ✓ Resists processing,
- ✓ Just wants highlights then likes to act quickly
- ✓ Becomes impatient, irritated, and feels over-loaded with details.

BOTH want to assess situations and then act. High score does it after analyzing a lot before-hand. Low score goes into action with very little analyzing.

3. EMOTIONAL EXPRESSIVENESS

At-a-Glance

Visible amount of emotion expressed in the moment.
Physical Attribute: Size of Eye Iris compared to white.

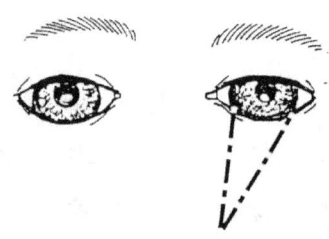

HIGH SCORE

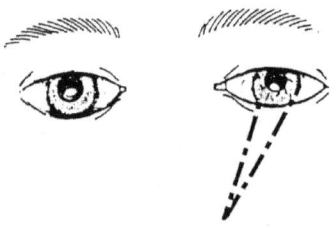

LOW SCORE

High Score

✓ Expresses emotions easily; laughs, cries, etc.

- ✓ Easily hurt by slights, disinterest, coldness, ignored.
- ✓ Needs emotional reassurances to feel warm, caring.
- ✓ May appear reactive, insincere since their emotions change quickly. Makes decisions and acts from mood of moment

Low Score

- ✓ Suppress sharing their feelings.
- ✓ Approaches situations logically.
- ✓ Uneasy with others' public display of feelings.
- ✓ Does not cry, laugh, anger spontaneously.
- ✓ Feelings are held within and are controlled.

BOTH want to: appropriately express emotions.
High score easily expresses whatever they feel.
Low score expresses thoughts rather than feelings.

4. TOLERANCE

At-a-Glance

Timing of emotional response to what is seen or heard
Physical Attribute: spacing between the eyes.

HIGH SCORE

LOW SCORE

High Score

✓ Slow to react
✓ Broadminded; overview preferred
✓ More easygoing; flexible
✓ Permissive, relaxed, laid back; appear inefficient

✓ Often procrastinates, excuses self, others; late.

Low Score

✓ Reacts quickly, urgently
✓ Follows commitments to letter of law;
✓ Quickly upset, irritated, intolerant
✓ Tries to control situations, people to get things right
✓ Feels pressure to get things done
✓ Strong on commitments

BOTH scores want to appropriately respond emotionally to what is seen or sensed.
High score takes longer.
Low score takes very little time.

5. SELF CONFIDENCE
At-a-Glance

Feeling of adequacy in new situations.
Physical Attribute: Broadness of face through eye sockets.

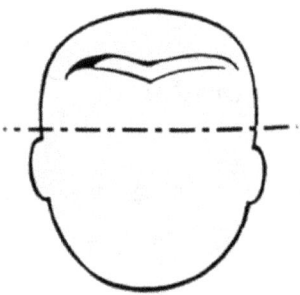

HIGH SCORE

LOW SCORE

High Score

- ✓ Easily assumes authority, responsibility without preparing
- ✓ Thinks, acts, on large scale; broader perspective
- ✓ Appears bossy, take charge attitude; inflexible, arrogant
- ✓ Feels confident in new situations
- ✓ Works better in leading roles
- ✓ Doesn't feel emotionally limited

Low Score

- ✓ Hesitates to take responsibility without preparing; doubts own authority
- ✓ Thinks and acts on smaller scale
- ✓ Appears indecisive, unable to act
- ✓ Feels hesitant in new situations
- ✓ Works well in supportive roles
- ✓ Always aware of own limitations

BOTH want to feel adequate responding in new situations.
High score assumes authority; acts without preparing. Low score needs preparation time before acting.

6. SELF RELIANCE
At-a-Glance

Basic reliance upon self.
Physical Attribute: flared nostrils.

HIGH SCORE

LOW SCORE

High Score

- ✓ Wants to make own decisions
- ✓ Likes to do things their own way
- ✓ Difficulty delegating authority
- ✓ Resists following instructions

✓ Independent in their thinking

Low Score

✓ Looks to others for info and opinions
✓ Seeks out advice of others for decision
✓ Cooperatively takes orders
✓ Willing to follow instructions
✓ Reticent about own convictions

BOTH want to depend on reliable source for decision-making.
High score relies on inside self.
Low relies upon outside sources.

7. VERBAL STYLE
At-a-Glance

High vs. Low

HIGH SCORE

LOW SCORE

High Score

- ✓ Uses more words
- ✓ Expresses more fully
- ✓ Forms thoughts while talking
- ✓ Repeat themselves
- ✓ Takes time getting to their point
- ✓ Appears rambling
- ✓ Appears to be aimless, wordy

Low Score

- ✓ Uses fewer words
- ✓ Expresses concisely
- ✓ Forms thoughts first, then speak
- ✓ Streamlines words
- ✓ Comes to point quickly
- ✓ Appears curt, brief
- ✓ May appear uninterested

BOTH want to appropriately express thoughts. High score forms thoughts as they speak with more words.
Low score uses few words; forms thoughts before speaking.

8. PHYSICAL INSULATION

At-a-Glance

Timing of response to outside stimulus (environment). Physical Attribute: first layer of skin (thickness, texture) and hair.

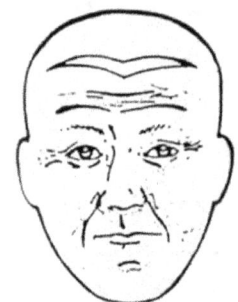

HIGH SCORE

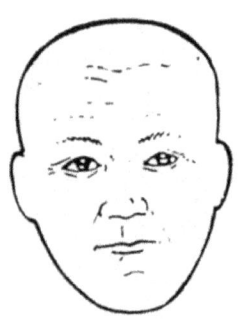

LOW SCORE

High Score

- ✓ Skin texture coarse, thick; deep lines and pores show.
- ✓ Insulated from outside world; takes lot to get to them
- ✓ Emotionally and physically rugged
- ✓ Vigorous tastes and expressions from all senses
- ✓ Want greater input of all senses
- ✓ Takes more stimuli to reach them

Low Score

- ✓ Skin texture thin, delicate; smooth, fine hair
- ✓ Affected easily by everything in outside environment;
- ✓ Physically and emotionally very sensitive
- ✓ Prefer quieter tastes, expressions, refinements
- ✓ Want less input of all senses
- ✓ Takes less stimuli to affect them

BOTH want to respond appropriately to the outside stimuli.
High score does it slower and with greater input.
Low score does it quickly with less input.

9. ADMINISTRATIVENESS

At-a-Glance

A keen sense and concern for material values.
Physical Attribute: Highly arched bridge of nose.

HIGH SCORE

LOW SCORE

High Score

✓ Knows the value of material things

- ✓ Expects to be paid their worth and knows value of
- ✓ Good administrator of time, energy, money
- ✓ Secures services rather than becoming personally involved
- ✓ May appear uncaring cold and impersonal.

Low Score

- ✓ Instinctively focuses on human values
- ✓ Spontaneously offers to personally help others
- ✓ Gives service without expecting payment
- ✓ Not realistic about time, energy, money
- ✓ Often lets others' demands and needs take priority and disregards their own
- ✓ Doesn't place monetary value on their services

BOTH want to be of service.
High score secures others to perform needed services. Low score personally performs the needed services.

10. THINKING STYLE

At-a-Glance

Type and Timing of Mental Process with new info.
Physical Attribute: Forehead: H= vertical L=sloped.

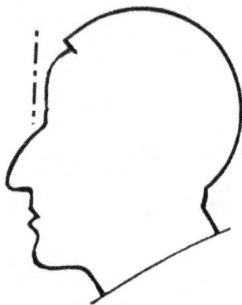

HIGH SCORE

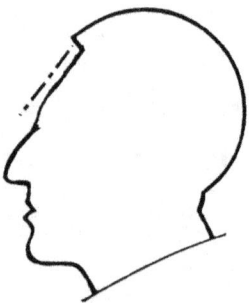

LOW SCORE

High Score

✓ Processes more slowly, in logical, sequential manner.

- ✓ Needs more time, orderly repetition to absorb unknown.
- ✓ Clarity diminishes quickly if stressed.
- ✓ Easily become overwhelmed if overloaded.
- ✓ Once info is learned, it's retained very well.

Low Score

- ✓ Processes new info quickly, applying the past (back brain) to new present situation.
- ✓ Appears as fast, smart thinker, but often misses processing parts because of reactive speed.
- ✓ Tends to interrupt, hurry others along, appears impatient.
- ✓ Able to apply theory quickly to situations.

BOTH want to think, process and respond.
High score is slow, subjective and sequential.
Low score is quick, objective and reactive.

11. CREDULITY

Tends to automatically accept things at face value.
Physical Attribute: Upturned nose (seen from profile)

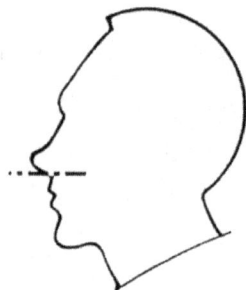

HIGH SCORE

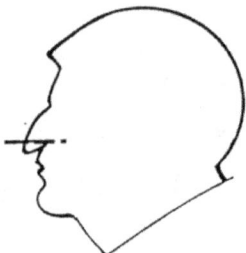

LOW SCORE

High Score

- ✓ Believes and accepts what is seen or heard
- ✓ Open minded; trusting, receptive

- ✓ Doesn't check things out and may innocently pass on faulty information
- ✓ Doesn't question or scrutinize or mistrust
- ✓ Easily taken advantage of because of their trusting nature, especially by loved ones

Low Score

- ✓ Tends to automatically doubt new things, people
- ✓ Scrutinizes and needs proof before accepting
- ✓ Appears closed minded and not open to new ideas
- ✓ Will not easily go along with change as they want proof of validity beforehand

BOTH want to appropriately accept new information. High score accepts without forethought. Low score accepts after forethought.

SUMMARY

At-a-Glance

We have briefly covered the main points of the individual traits of Discriminative, Analytical, Emotionality, Tolerance, Self-Confidence, Self-Reliance, Verbal Style, Physical Insulation, Administrative, Thinking, and Credulity.

These traits, however, are not isolated ABCs, but each trait is interactive with another trait and some traits will diminish the effect of another trait or it may amplify the effect of that trait.

Let's take the same traits we have covered individually and discover they augment or diminish each other on this overview chart so you can see At-A-Glance how they interact with and affect each other.

For example, if you have a high score on innate Self-Confidence and a high score on Self-Reliance and a high score on Physical Insulation, all these will work together to make an independent thinking, confident acting and emotionally and physically insulated person. They will automatically amplify each other and give more drive and independent nature to the personality.

If, on the other hand, you had a low score on innate Self-Confidence, a low score in Self-Reliance and you were very low on Physical Insulation, you would not be meeting new challenges as easily as everything would quickly be getting to you. You would be very sensitive to your environment as well as emotionally sensitive to criticism and you would be looking towards other people for your answers, rather than making up your own mind and not having the stamina and drive to see it through.

Now look at your face again. Just form the basic traits you have learned in this book, how many combinations can you put together on your own face and realize how they interact with each other. Notice which of your single traits tend to amplify and which tend to diminish the other traits.

You may now have a better appreciation of yourself and as you notice the combination of traits on other people's faces, you have a much deeper understanding of who they are and how you can best establish rapport, communicate effectively and create lasting loving relationships.

GLOSSARY

Administrative: High score is a good administrator; thinks in monetary values; utilizes other people to obtain services. Low score is focused primarily on human values; automatic helper; many times doesn't even think of monetary reciprocity for personal help or work they do.

Analytical: The need to process things before acting in any given situation. Timing of response it takes to act. High scores take longer because of need to process. Low scores are more direct action people and take much less time to process.

Credulity: The tendency to automatically take things at face value before proven. High score is open, trusting; believes first and accepts readily. Low score is much more skeptical; requires lots of proof beforehand. Automatically tends to doubt first.

Discriminative: timing of instinctive, emotional selectivity. High score is very selective about things in their life; constant distinctions; requires time and space to get to know people. Low score makes few distinctions upfront, has casual approach to life, easy to get to know, makes selections after involving self.

Emotional Expressiveness: Visible amount of emotion expressed in the moment. High score has lots of outflow of emotion; feelings are close to the surface; decisions are made from feelings, not head. Low score expresses little of what is felt; comfortable speaking logically; doesn't share or display emotions easily.

Physical Insulation: Timing of nerve response to outside stimuli from environment. High score= longer time, more of everything needed from outside to "get through to them." Low score = needs less of everything from outside to get to them; feelings hurt easily; personalizes things.

Self-Confidence: Feeling of adequacy in new situations. High score naturally feels very adequate and confident, thinks in big terms, more decisive, tends to "take over" situations. Low score feels more self-conscious in new situations, hesitates to perform without lots of preparation; earns their self-confidence through building from past successes; is a good support team member.

Self-Reliance: Basic instinctive reliance upon self. High score looks to self automatically for answers, makes own decisions without consulting others; resists instructions, independent thinker. Low score is a more reliant person, looks to others to help make decisions, willing to follow instructions.

Thinking Style: Type and timing of mental process. High score is a sequential thinker. Processes new information more slowly and sequentially; learns better by outline form and rote, retains better after several reviews; interested in the whole process; shuts down under pressure. Low score is an objective thinker. Fast reactive style of thinking; moves fast to act on what is seen or heard; often becomes impatient; tends to go off past experience and feelings; may miss some parts in speeding through new information.

Tolerance: Basic timing of emotional reaction to what is seen or heard. High score is slow to react emotionally; has broad view; more permissive, relaxed, procrastinates. Low score reacts quickly to what is more urgent; they try to control situations; keeps promises; doesn't bend rules.

Verbal Style: Style of expressing oneself verbally. High score uses many words, takes time getting to point; repeats self; tends to give listener whole story and form their thoughts as they are speaking. Low score expresses self concisely; uses streamlined sentences; gets right to the point; thinks first then speaks briefly.

About Author Annemarie

Annemarie has been in the "reading people" business since 1980. She is certified as presenter, trainer, consultant and personal counselor of this science. Her presentations are both practical and entertaining. The information is applicable to both personal and professional life. She has taught in Canada, Mexico, and Eastern Europe and throughout the United States. Her presentations have ranged from cruise ships in the Caribbean to Dale Carnegie Trainings in Mexico.

She has written numerous articles for newspapers, business journals and newsletters as well as many training manuals. Her children's storybook *Keesha and the Rainbow Parrot Guide,* and *the Guide Book,* a companion book for teachers and parents, teaches children how to appreciate themselves and understand other children that have different personalities.

Annemarie's guest appearances on TV, radio and talk shows have wide appeal as well as keynote speaker at universities and business conferences. Her two newspaper columns were always inspirational and touching in content. She designed and taught required graduate coursework at an Arizona educational institute. Trial attorneys hire her as consultant for jury selection and client prep for trials.

Annemarie loves working privately with individuals to master their minds, open their hearts and appreciate their natural gifts and talents. Her insightful compassionate nature empowers people to appreciate who they are, teaches them how to deal with people different from themselves and helps them to connect with and cherish the people in their life.

She is available for public speaking engagements, workshops, retreats, business consulting, and private sessions for individuals. She is certified through the Personology Institute to teach all levels of coursework for certification.

On the personal side:

She lives in a small mountain village in Arizona and travels for work and pleasure. She has previously published two poetry books, *Reaching for the Sun* and *Wisdom of the Heart,* with another near completion. Her upcoming book, *Hurrah for Humans,* tells her true-life stories that uplift the human spirit and show the goodness of humanity.

Annemarie enjoys nature, traveling, writing, photography, watercolors, hiking, kayaking, and natural healing. She cherishes family, good friends and is an active community supporter wherever she travels. She believes, "We are one in spirit, but express ourselves as unique individual human beings."

Contact information for
Annemarie Eveland, presenter, author:

Hurrah for Humans, LLC
P.O. Box 493
Pine, Arizona 85544-0493

Website: http://annemarieeveland.com
Blog: https://annemarieeveland.wordpress.com
Email: Annemarie@HurrahForHumans.com

MY PERSONAL NOTES

MY PERSONAL NOTES

MY PERSONAL NOTES

MY PERSONAL NOTES

MY PERSONAL NOTES

MY PERSONAL NOTES

MY PERSONAL NOTES